Beginning e-Textile Development

Prototyping e-Textiles with Wearic Smart Textiles Kit and the BBC micro:bit

Pradeeka Seneviratne

Apress®

Beginning e-Textile Development: Prototyping e-Textiles with Wearic Smart Textiles Kit and the BBC micro:bit

Pradeeka Seneviratne
Mulleriyawa, Sri Lanka

ISBN-13 (pbk): 978-1-4842-6260-3   ISBN-13 (electronic): 978-1-4842-6261-0
https://doi.org/10.1007/978-1-4842-6261-0

Managing Director, Apress Media LLC: Welmoed Spahr
Acquisitions Editor: Natalie Pao
Development Editor: James Markham
Coordinating Editor: Jessica Vakili

Distributed to the book trade worldwide by Springer Science+Business Media New York, 1 NY Plaza, New York, NY 10014. Phone 1-800-SPRINGER, fax (201) 348-4505, e-mail orders-ny@springer-sbm.com, or visit www.springeronline.com. Apress Media, LLC is a California LLC and the sole member (owner) is Springer Science + Business Media Finance Inc (SSBM Finance Inc). SSBM Finance Inc is a Delaware corporation.

For information on translations, please e-mail booktranslations@springernature.com; for reprint, paperback, or audio rights, please e-mail bookpermissions@springernature.com.

Apress titles may be purchased in bulk for academic, corporate, or promotional use. eBook versions and licenses are also available for most titles. For more information, reference our Print and eBook Bulk Sales web page at http://www.apress.com/bulk-sales.

Any source code or other supplementary material referenced by the author in this book is available to readers on GitHub via the book's product page, located at www.apress.com/978-1-4842-6260-3. For more detailed information, please visit http://www.apress.com/source-code.

Printed on acid-free paper

Table of Contents

About the Author

Pradeeka Seneviratne is a graduate from the Sri Lanka Institute of Information Technology (SLIIT). He has nearly two decades of experience working on large and complex IT projects in the industrial world. Pradeeka has focused on different technologies and software in a variety of fields and roles, such as programmer, analyst, architect, and team leader. He has also authored several maker-related books, including *Beginning BBC micro:bit* (Apress), *Beginning LoRa Radio Networks with Arduino* (Apress), and *Building Arduino PLCs* (Apress).

About the Technical Reviewers

Rebecca Stewart is a lecturer in the School of Electronic Engineering and Computer Science at Queen Mary University of London where she completed her PhD in 2010. She works with e-textiles and signal processing to build interactive, body-centric wearable computing systems, often incorporating performance, fashion, music, and/or design. In 2011, she co-founded Codasign, an arts technology company that taught children and adults how to use code and electronics in creative projects. She regularly collaborates with artists and fashion designers and has had work featured by the BBC, *New York Times*, and NPR.

Thomas Fröis is the founder and CEO of TEXIBLE GmbH. He graduated from Vorarlberg University of Applied Sciences in engineering and management with a specialization in product management. Thomas won the Innovation Award from the state of Vorarlberg in 2016 and was nominated for the startup challenge Aveneo in 2017.

CHAPTER 1

Getting Started

Wearable electronics fall into anything that can be worn on the body. Alternatively, you can refer to them as "wearable technology," "wearables," "fashion technology," "tech togs," or "fashion electronics." Wearable electronics accessories can be built with or without using microcontrollers. However, microcontrollers allow wearable electronic accessories to provide a rich set of features to users.

You can wear them by attaching to your clothes, close to the surface of the skin, or on the surface of the skin. They can detect, analyze, and transmit information concerning, as an example, body signals such as vital signs and ambient data, which allow in some cases immediate biofeedback to the wearer.

Wearable devices such as activity trackers are an example of the Internet of Things since **"things"** such as electronics, software, sensors, and connectivity are effectors that enable objects to exchange data through the Internet with a manufacturer, operator, and/or other connected devices, without requiring human intervention.

Wearable technology has a variety of applications that grow as the field itself expands. It appears prominently in consumer electronics with the popularization of the smartwatch and activity tracker. Apart from commercial uses, wearable technology is being incorporated into navigation systems, advanced textiles, and healthcare.

You are already aware that this book guides how to make wearable electronics prototypes. A prototype is a simulation or sample version of a final product, which is used for testing prior to launch. A prototype could

© Pradeeka Seneviratne 2020
P. Seneviratne, *Beginning e-Textile Development*,
https://doi.org/10.1007/978-1-4842-6261-0_1

be bulky, heavy, or have a lot of wires that make you uncomfortable. But it will provide you a "proof" about how it works after you build the product with most suitable components (as an example, you can use the Wearic textile heating element to prototype a heated glove, but you can replace it with another heating pad when in production).

This chapter will help you to get started with your Wearic Smart Textiles Kit. It will also set the stage for the experiments and projects you will find in the following chapters.

1.1 Choosing a Development Board

A development board is basically a printed circuit board (PCB) with circuitry and hardware on board to facilitate experimentation with certain microcontrollers. These development boards facilitate you to connect sensors and actuators. Also, they may have built-in sensors, communication interfaces, Internet connectivity, buttons, debugging LEDs, and so forth.

There are hundreds of development boards available in the market. Arduino, Raspberry Pi, BeagleBone, and the BBC micro:bit are some of the popular microcontrollers among makers and electronic hobbyists for their everyday projects. Most of them are cheap, but a few of them are expensive. As an example, the Arduino and micro:bit are cheap, but the BeagleBone Black is expensive. So we will choose the BBC micro:bit because it is one of the popular microcontrollers for prototyping things.

1.2 The BBC micro:bit

The micro:bit is a pocket-sized microcontroller board designed by the BBC for use in computer education in the United Kingdom, but now it is becoming increasingly popular with students and makers around the world.

Before you start coding with the micro:bit, you should be familiar with the key features of the board.

Figure 1-1 shows the front of the micro:bit board. The front of the board has two pushbuttons, an LED display, and an edge connector.

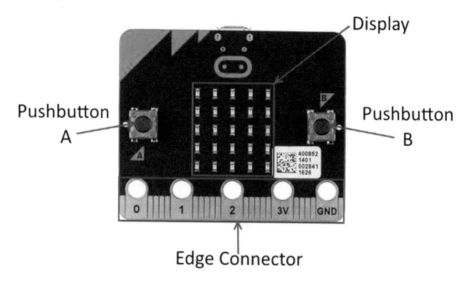

Figure 1-1. *Front view of the micro:bit*

The following list explains the most important things that can be found on the front of the board:

1. **Two pushbuttons** – These are momentary pushbuttons labeled A and B that allow you to directly interact with your programs. For example, you can configure them to control a game or pause and skip songs on a playlist.

2. **Display** – The display consists of 25 surface-mounted red LEDs arranged as a 5 × 5 grid that allows you to display text, images, and animations. This 5 × 5 LED display can be used as an ambient light sensor too.

3. **Edge connector** – The total of 25 pins on the edge connector allows you to connect various sensors and actuators, access I/O lines, and connect to power and ground. These pins allow you to access the LED matrix, two pushbuttons, I2C bus, and SPI (Serial Peripheral Interface). The 0, 1, 2, 3V, and GND pins are exposed as ring connectors, which allow you to easily connect alligator cables/crocodile clips. An edge connector breakout board can be used to access all 25 pins.

The following list explains the most important things that can be found on the back of the board (Figure 1-2):

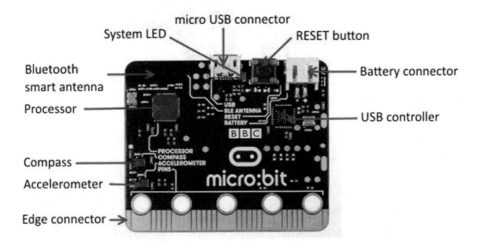

***Figure 1-2.** Back view of the micro:bit*

1. **Processor (Nordic nRF51822)** – 16 MHz 32-bit ARM Cortex-M0 CPU, 256 KB flash memory, and 16 KB static RAM with 2.4 GHz Bluetooth Low Energy wireless networking, which allows you to pair the micro:bit with Bluetooth-enabled mobile devices running Android and iOS.

2. **Compass (NXP/Freescale MAG3110)** – Allows you to measure magnetic field strength in each of three axes.

3. **Accelerometer (NXP/Freescale MMA8652)** – Allows you to measure the acceleration and movement along three axes.

Note   There are two versions of the micro:bit board. Newer micro:bits have a combined compass and accelerometer chip, and the previous version has separate chips. However, both versions work exactly the same way.

---

4. **USB controller (NXP/Freescale KL26Z)** – 48 MHz ARM Cortex-M0+ core microcontroller, which includes a full-speed USB 2.0 On-the-Go (OTG) controller, used as a communication interface between the USB and the main Nordic microcontroller.

5. **Micro USB connector** – Allows you to connect the micro:bit with a computer to flashing code or power it with USB power.

6. **Bluetooth smart antenna** – A printed antenna that transmits Bluetooth signals in the 2.4 GHz band.

7. **RESET button** – Allows you to reset the micro:bit and restart the currently running program or bring the micro:bit into maintenance mode.

8. **Battery connector/socket** – Allows you to power the micro:bit with two AAA/AA batteries.

9. **System LED** – The yellow color LED indicates USB power (solid) and data transfer (flashing). It doesn't indicate the battery power.

10. **Edge connector** – Includes 25 pins.

1.3 micro:bit Inputs and Outputs

The micro:bit exposes its I/O pins through the edge connector as shown in Figure 1-3. The edge connector consists of large and small connection pads (pins).

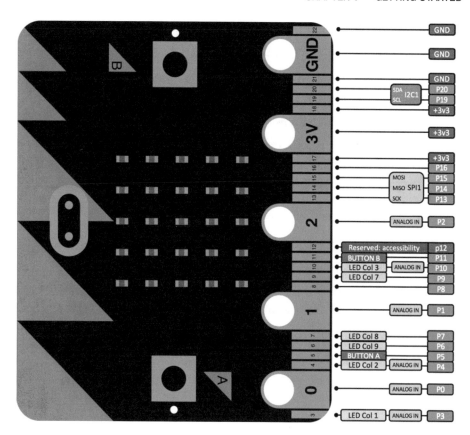

Figure 1-3. *Types of pins and usage (image courtesy of the micro:bit foundation:* `http://microbit.org/`*)*

The five large connection pads expose GPIO pins 0, 1, 2, 3V, and GND, respectively. You can easily attach alligator leads to these large pads. The following are the functions of the large pins:

- **0** – GPIO (general-purpose digital input and output) with analog to digital converter (ADC).

- **1** – GPIO (general-purpose digital input and output) with analog to digital converter (ADC).

- **2** – GPIO (general-purpose digital input and output) with analog to digital converter (ADC).

- **3V** – 3.3 V regulated power output or power input. If the micro:bit is powered by USB or a battery, then you can use the 3V pin as a power output to power other peripherals. If the micro:bit is not being powered by USB or a battery, you can use the 3V pin as a power input to power the micro:bit.

- **GND** – Ground.

There are 20 small pads numbered from 3 to 22. You cannot attach alligator leads to them because these pins are very narrow. You need an edge connector breakout to access these pins. The following are the functions of the small pins (source: `https://makecode.microbit.org/device/pins`):

- **Pin 3** – GPIO shared with LED Column 1 of the LED screen. This pin can be used for ADC and digital I/O when the LED screen is turned off.

- **Pin 4** – GPIO shared with LED Column 2 of the LED screen. This pin can be used for ADC and digital I/O when the LED screen is turned off.

- **Pin 5** – GPIO shared with button A. This lets you trigger or detect a button "A" click externally. This pin has a pull-up resistor, which means that by default it is at the voltage of 3 V. To replace button A on the micro:bit with an external button, connect one end of the external button to pin 5 and the other end to GND. When the button is pressed, the voltage on pin 5 is pulled down to 0, which generates a button click event.

- **Pin 6** – GPIO shared with LED Column 9 of the LED screen. This pin can be used for digital I/O when the LED screen is turned off.

- **Pin 7** – GPIO shared with LED Column 8 of the LED screen. This pin can be used for digital I/O when the LED screen is turned off.

- **Pin 8** – Dedicated GPIO, for sending and sensing digital signals.

- **Pin 9** – GPIO shared with LED Column 7 of the LED screen. This pin can be used for digital I/O when the LED screen is turned off.

- **Pin 10** – GPIO shared with LED Column 3 of the LED screen. This pin can be used for ADC and digital I/O when the LED screen is turned off.

- **Pin 11** – GPIO shared with button B. This lets you trigger or detect a button "B" click externally.

- **Pin 12** – This GPIO pin has been reserved to provide accessibility support.

- **Pin 13** – GPIO that is conventionally used for the serial clock (SCK) signal of the three-wire Serial Peripheral Interface (SPI) bus.

- **Pin 14** – GPIO that is conventionally used for the Master In Slave Out (MISO) signal of the SPI bus.

- **Pin 15** – GPIO that is conventionally used for the Master Out Slave In (MOSI) signal of the SPI bus.

- **Pin 16** – Dedicated GPIO (conventionally also used for the SPI "Chip Select" function).

- **Pins 17 and 18** – These pins are wired to the 3V supply, like the large "3V" pad.

- **Pins 19 and 20** – Implement the clock signal (SCL) and the data line (SDA) of the I2C bus communication protocol. With I2C, several devices can be connected on the same bus and send/read messages to/from the CPU. Internally, the accelerometer and the compass are connected to I2C.

- **Pins 21 and 22** – These pins are wired to the GND pin and serve no other function.

1.4 Buying a micro:bit

You can buy a micro:bit board from various local and online sellers. The following list includes some of the online sellers that typically stock the micro:bit along with the product page. These sellers usually ship the micro:bit to any country in the world:

- **SparkFun** – www.sparkfun.com/products/14208

- **Adafruit** – www.adafruit.com/product/3530

- **Kitronik** – https://kitronik.co.uk/collections/microbit-accessories/products/5613-bbc-microbit-board-only

- **Seeed Studio** – www.seeedstudio.com/micro-bit-p-2886.html

Starter kits usually provide everything you need to connect the micro:bit to your computer and power it with batteries. A starter kit typically includes the following parts:

- micro:bit

- Micro USB cable

- Battery holder

- Two AAA batteries (optional)

The following is a list of sellers that offer starter kits at competitive prices:

- **SparkFun micro:bit Go Bundle** – www.sparkfun.com/ products/14336

- **Adafruit BBC micro:bit Go Bundle** – www.adafruit. com/product/3362

- **Kitronik BBC micro:bit Starter Kit** – https:// kitronik.co.uk/products/5615-bbc-microbit- starter-kit?_pos=2&_sid=015c88a44&_ss=r

Batteries and Battery Holders

You need two zinc-carbon or alkaline batteries to power the micro:bit. SparkFun stocks good-quality battery cases for two AAA batteries.

This battery holder has a power switch, color-coded power leads, and a JST-PH connector. You can purchase it by visiting www.sparkfun.com/ products/15101.

You can also find similar battery holders from the following sellers:

- **Adafruit** – www.adafruit.com/product/4191

- **Kitronik** – https://kitronik.co.uk/collections/
microbit-accessories/products/2271-2xaaa-
battery-cage-with-jst-connector

USB Cable

You need a USB micro-B cable to connect the micro:bit to a computer. This is the same cable usually bundled with many mobile phones and some consumer electronic products. You can purchase a cable from the following sellers:

- **SparkFun** – www.sparkfun.com/products/13244.

- **Adafruit** – www.adafruit.com/product/592

- **Kitronik** – https://kitronik.co.uk/collections/
microbit-accessories/products/4154-1m-usb-type-
a-to-micro-b-usb-noodle-cable

- **Seeed Studio** – www.seeedstudio.com/Micro-USB-
Cable-48cm-p-1475.html

Alligator Leads

You will need a few alligator leads with different colors to build prototypes without soldering wires with the micro:bit edge connector. You can purchase a bundle for alligator leads from the following sellers:

- **MonkMakes** – www.monkmakes.com/mb-alligator-
short.html

- **SparkFun** – www.sparkfun.com/products/12978

- **Adafruit** – www.adafruit.com/product/1008

- **Kitronik** – https://kitronik.co.uk/products/
  2407-crocodile-leads-pack-of-10?_pos=1&_sid=
  7f8d56aca&_ss=r

1.5 Coding the micro:bit

Microsoft MakeCode is a web-based online editor that allows you to build programs using snappable blocks. It is also known as a graphical programming language and supports all modern web browsers and platforms.

You don't need a user account to create and save projects with MakeCode. All projects are saved in your web browser's local cache.

Note   MakeCode is based on the open source project Microsoft Programming Experience Toolkit (PXT), and its framework is available at https://github.com/Microsoft/pxt. MakeCode provides environments such as BBC micro:bit, Adafruit Circuit Playground Express, Minecraft, LEGO MINDSTORMS Education EV3, Cue, Chibi Chip, and Grove Zero.

The web-based editor has the following sections and controls:

- **Simulator** – Provides the output without the real hardware while you are building the code. The following buttons can be used to control the behavior of the simulator (Figure 1-4):

  - **Start/stop the simulator** – Stops the program and restarts from the beginning.

- **Restart the simulator** – Restarts the program (output) from the beginning.

- **Toggle debug mode** – Allows you to run the code in debug mode. You can add breakpoints to your code and run the code step by step.

- **Mute audio** – Mutes audio when you are working with music and speech.

- **Launch in full screen** – Shows the simulator in full-screen mode.

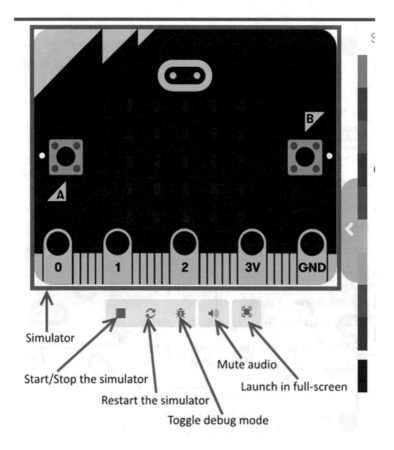

Figure 1-4. *The simulator and control buttons*

- **Toolbox** – Provides "blocks" categories. Also allows you to search extensions in the toolbox and add more extensions (packages) to the toolbox if available (Figure 1-5).

Figure 1-5. *Blocks categories and blocks. As an example, the Input category consists of blocks "on button A pressed," "on shake," "on pin P0 pressed," and so on*

- **Coding area** – The area you use to build the code with blocks and write the code with JavaScript (Figure 1-6).

Figure 1-6. *The coding area. It shows "forever" and "on start" blocks by default*

- **Editor controls** (Figure 1-7):

  - **Home** – Takes you to the home screen (https://makecode.microsoft.org/), which shows recent projects and other activities.

  - **Share** – Displays the Share Project window that lets you publish your project to the public cloud and embed your project into a web page with different options.

  - **Blocks or JavaScript** – Allows you to switch the code view from Blocks to JavaScript or back again. Click one of the view buttons at the top center of the window.

16

- **Help** – Shows a menu with help options such as support, reference, blocks, JavaScript, hardware, and where to buy.

- **Cogwheel** – Allows you to access project settings, adding extensions, deleting the current project, deleting all the projects, choosing a language, and pairing micro:bit for one-click download.

- **Undo and redo** – Allows you to undo and redo recent changes you make either in Blocks or JavaScript in the bottom right of the editor window.

- **Zoom in and zoom out** – When you are working in the Blocks view, the zoom buttons change the size of the blocks. When you are working with the code in the JavaScript view, the zoom buttons change the size of the text.

- **Save project** – You can rename your project. The disk icon can be used to save the project and download the hex file of the project.

- **Download** – The Download button will download a compiled version of the code (hex file) onto your computer.

- **Create GitHub repository** – Allows you to host your code on GitHub and work together with friends.

- **Show/hide the simulator** – The show/hide the simulator button can be used to show or hide the simulator.

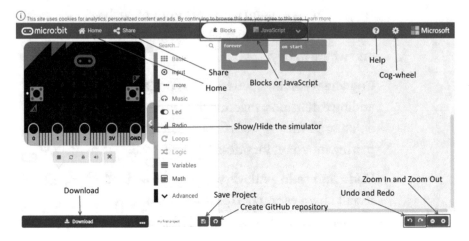

Figure 1-7. *Editor controls*

1.6 Setting Up the Workspace

First, you will need to set up the workspace for your project. The following steps explain to you how to do that:

- Using your web browser, go to `https://makecode.microbit.org/`.

- Under **My Projects**, choose **New Project** (Figure 1-8).

Figure 1-8. *New Project button*

- In the **Create a Project** dialog box, type in a name for your project. Then click the **Create** button (Figure 1-9).

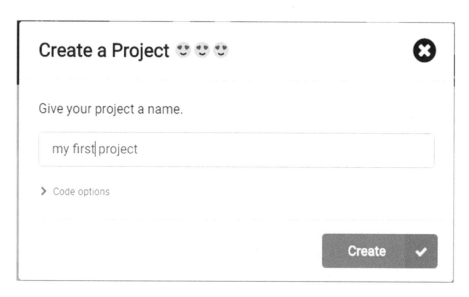

Figure 1-9. *Providing a name for the project*

- Your project will create, and a workspace for your project will load onto the page (Figure 1-10).

Figure 1-10. *MakeCode workspace for the micro:bit*

1.7 Downloading an Extension

To build code for some projects, you may need to download extension(s)/
package(s) onto your MakeCode project. An extension is a set of blocks
that provides functions that the core micro:bit library doesn't have. An
example is the **neopixel** extension (`https://makecode.microbit.org/`
`pkg/microsoft/pxt-neopixel`). This library provides a set of blocks to
make various lighting patterns and lighting effects with WS2812B-based
NeoPixels.

Follow these steps when you require to use additional extensions not
included with the MakeCode editor by default:

- Choose the **cogwheel** icon in the top right of the
  window. Then, from the drop-down menu, choose
  Extensions (Figure 1-11).

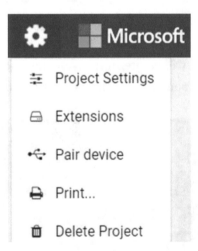

Figure 1-11. *The "**More...**" menu provides useful options related to
your project*

- In the **Extensions** page, type the name of the extension you want to search (e.g., weatherbit). Then press **Enter** or click the **Search** button. You will get a list of extensions/packages based on your search (Figure 1-12).

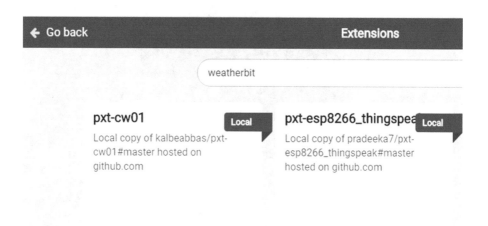

Figure 1-12. *Searching for an extension*

- From the search results, choose the extension/package you want to download (Figure 1-13).

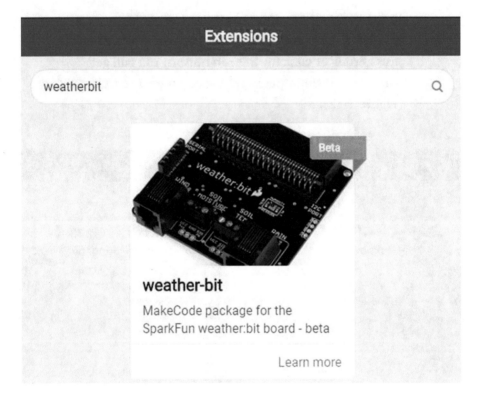

Figure 1-13. *Choosing an extension*

- The extension/package will download onto the
  MakeCode. After that, you can find it in the toolbox
  (Figure 1-14).

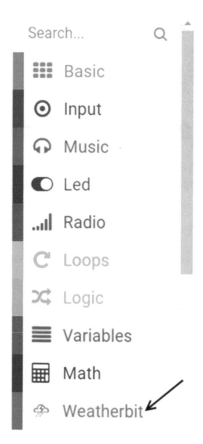

Figure 1-14. *Downloaded extension*

1.8 Downloading a Hex File onto Your Computer

After building the code, you should compile it first. The compiled version of the code is known as the hex file.

Click the **Download** button at the bottom of the window. A hex file will download onto your computer. The word "**microbit**" will prepend to the file name. Also, each **space** in the file name will replace with the **hyphen** mark. As an example, if you have a project named **Hello World**, the name of the downloaded hex file would be **microbit-Hello-World**.

Files you have downloaded are usually saved in the **Downloads** folder of your computer. Some web browsers allow you to change the default location to save the downloaded files.

1.9 Flashing a Hex File onto the micro:bit

The process of copying a **hex file** (the compiled version of code) onto the micro:bit is called **flashing**. The LED on the back of your micro:bit flashes during the file copying. Once this has been completed, the micro:bit will automatically restart and start executing your code:

- Connect the micro:bit to your computer using a micro USB cable.

- A new drive will appear named **MICROBIT**. This is called the **micro:bit drive**.

- Drag and drop the downloaded hex file onto the micro:bit drive (Figure 1-15). Usually, in a Windows-based system, you can find the downloaded file in the **Downloads** folder.

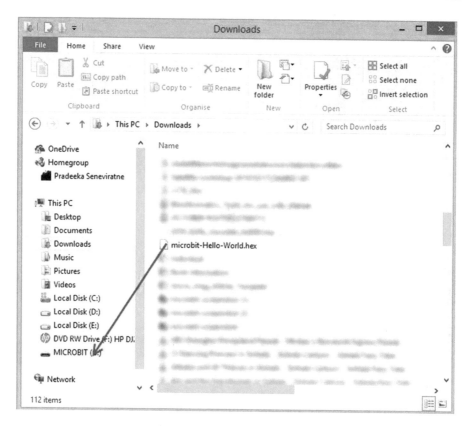

Figure 1-15. *Copying a hex file onto the micro:bit drive using Windows Explorer*

- Some web browsers allow you to drag and drop the downloaded hex file directly from the browser's **Download Bar** (Figure 1-16).

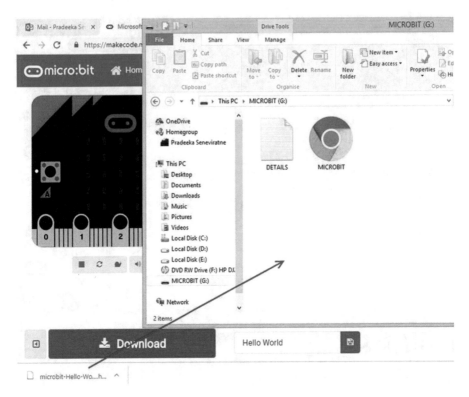

Figure 1-16. *Copying a hex file onto the micro:bit drive using Google Chrome's Download Bar*

1.10 Opening a Shared Project

This book presents shared URLs for all the MakeCode projects. These URLs allow you to import MakeCode projects to your workspace for editing. The following steps explain how to access the shared project, **https://makecode.microbit.org/_4607DHVHbK2V:**

- Type or paste the shared project URL in your web browser's address bar and then press **Enter** (Figure 1-17).

Figure 1-17. *Shared project URL*

- The project will open in the web browser as a read-only project (Figure 1-18).

Figure 1-18. *Project in read-only mode*

- Click the **Edit Code** button (Figure 1-19).

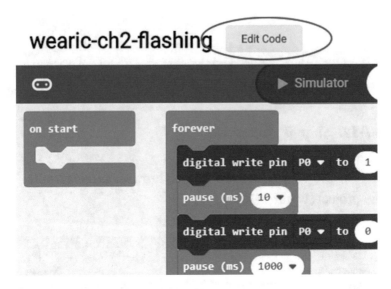

Figure 1-19. *Switching to the edit mode*

- The project will open with the MakeCode editor
  and automatically add to your browser's local cache
  (Figure 1-20).

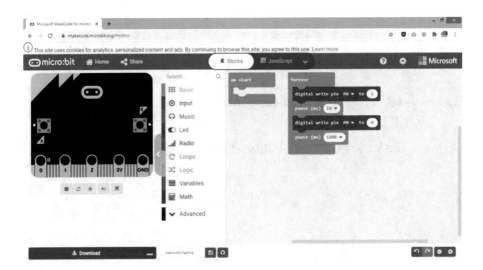

Figure 1-20. *The MakeCode editor*

Now you can edit the project or rename it, or you can do whatever you want with it.

1.11 Powering the micro:bit

The micro:bit requires 3.3 V clean power supply. You can use two AAA-sized or two AA-sized batteries to power the micro:bit through the battery connector on the back of the board. You can also use the USB power to power the micro:bit through the micro USB connector on the back of the board. The USB controller chip will automatically convert the 5 V USB power to 3.3 V.

Note   The micro:bit can also be powered via the 3V pad on the edge connector, but this may not be suitable for beginners.

Let's have a look at these two powering options in more detail.

Battery Power

If you need a portable, long-term, and cheap power source, you can probably go for the AAA or AA battery power and a suitable battery holder with a connector. The following steps explain to you how to connect your micro:bit with a AAA battery power:

- Take the battery holder and two batteries.

- Place two batteries into the battery holder.

- Pinch together the two wires at the base of the connector and push into the battery connector on the back of the micro:bit.

Note   You can also use two D-type batteries to power the micro:bit. These batteries are heavy and take large space, therefore not suitable for wearable projects.

USB Power

You can use the USB power as the basic option to power your micro:bit. You can get USB power from many sources: desktop computers, laptops, USB chargers for phones and cameras, TVs, and many more. The following steps explain to you how to connect your micro:bit correctly to a USB power source:

1. Take a micro USB cable (Type-A to Micro-B).

2. Push the small plug of the micro USB cable into the USB connector on the back of the micro:bit.

3. Push the large plug of the micro USB cable into the USB port on your computer.

1.12 The Wearic Smart Textiles Kit

It is never so easy to make your own innovative sensor textile and wear it. The Wearic Smart Textiles Kit (Figure 1-21) is an e-textile development platform that allows you to build smart textile prototypes. It saves time and cost and allows you to prototype your solution and test it.

From heated cloth to weight measurement in chairs, there are no limits to your creativity and your projects.

The kit includes the following things:

- Wearic expansion board for Nano V3.0 Atmel Atmega328

- 1 × spool conductive yarn, silver-coated 235/36dtex, 20 m

- 1 × needle

- 2 × sewable LED module, blue and white

- 1 × Wearic textile pressure sensor

- 1 × Wearic textile push-button double

- 1 × Wearic LED textile double

- 1 × Wearic textile heating

- 1 × Wearic textile wetness sensor

- 1 × isolation non-woven with adhesive coating, 30 × 30 cm

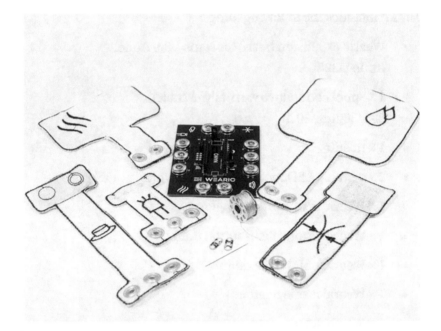

Figure 1-21. *Wearic Smart Textiles Kit*

Note   This book does not use the Wearic **expansion board** to build the projects.

You can purchase a **Wearic Smart Textiles Kit** directly from *www.wearic.com/product/smart-textiles-kit/*.

You will learn about each Wearic textile element in the proceeding chapters.

1.13 Summary

In this chapter, you learned about the hardware and software platforms you are going to use to build the e-textile prototypes. You also learned how to use the micro:bit with the MakeCode online editor.

CHAPTER 2

Working with LEDs

LEDs are widely used in the trendy fashion industry to make amazing glowing garments. However, they appear mostly in high-tech fashion shows and luxury events. These LED garments are highly expensive, but if you know the engineering behind them, you can make one for just a few dollars.

These LED sequins can be used not to just glow your garments with different lighting effects. You can also use them as indicators to indicate proximities, wireless connection statuses (Bluetooth, WiFi, LoRa, etc.), a different type of mood (happy, sad, etc.), and thresholds, to visualize sensor values or sensor statuses, as active lighting for more safety at night, and anything imaginable via conjunction with other sensors.

These LED sequins do not generate heat as incandescent bulbs do. They give off superbright light but virtually no heat. They are battery operated and consume much less current. Hence, they are very safe to wear with your garments.

In this chapter, you will learn how to add sewable LED sequins to your textiles and control them using the micro:bit to make amazing lighting effects.

© Pradeeka Seneviratne 2020
P. Seneviratne, *Beginning e-Textile Development*,
https://doi.org/10.1007/978-1-4842-6261-0_2

2.1 The LED Textile Element

The Wearic LED textile element is a piece of fabric developed with LEDs
and conductive threads (Figure 2-1). It originally comes without sewed
LEDs on it and requires you to sew them using conductive threads. The
LED textile has three snap connectors to connect it with other textiles or a
PCB (printed circuit board) with female snap connectors.

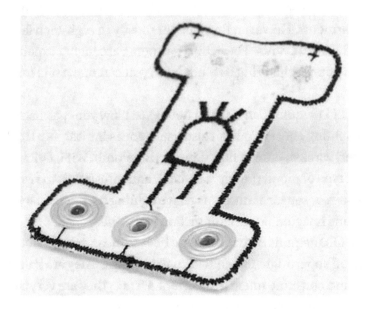

Figure 2-1. *The Wearic LED textile element*

The Wearic LED textile comes with two LED sequins (white and blue)
which you can sew onto the LED textile element (Figure 2-2).

Figure 2-2. *LED textile element, two sewable LED sequins (blue and white), conductive thread (silver yarn), and needle*

The **LED textile element** has two sides: The **top** of the LED textile element (Figure 2-3) has a machine-embroidered **LED symbol**. You can also see two pairs of circular pads (sewed with silver yarns) for sewing LED sequins. The circular silver pads are embroidered and connected to the snap connectors. The positive pads for each LED are marked with the plus sign. When you sew the LEDs, make sure that you place the "+" sign on the LED over the "+" sign on the textile. The two center pads are negative.

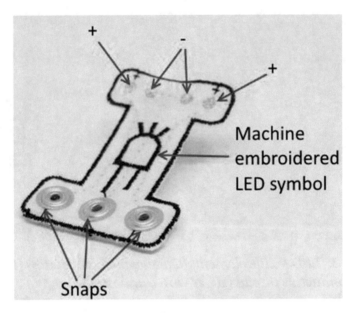

Figure 2-3. *Top of the LED textile element*

The **bottom** of the textile LED element (Figure 2-4) is isolated with a piece of fabric to cover the backside of the machine embroidery. That protects the silver yarn against short circuits. The fabric is a polyester non-woven.

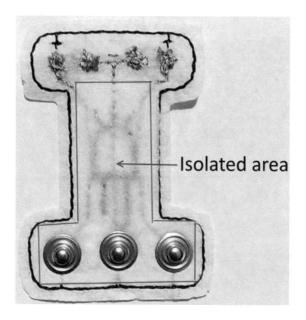

Figure 2-4. *Bottom of the LED textile element*

2.2 Testing LED Sequins Using the micro:bit Power

The Wearic LED textile comes with two sewable LED sequins (LilyPad LEDs) in two colors: blue and white. A sewable LED sequin can be lit using a 3–6 V DC power supply. Your micro:bit can provide 3.3 V clean (regulated) power through the 3V pin when you connect it to USB or 2 × AAA battery power.

Here are the **"forward voltages"** of each LED:

- **Blue LED** – 3.2 volts

- **White LED** – 3.3 volts

Just connect an LED sequin to the micro:bit using the alligator cables as shown in Figure 2-5. Your LED sequin should light up.

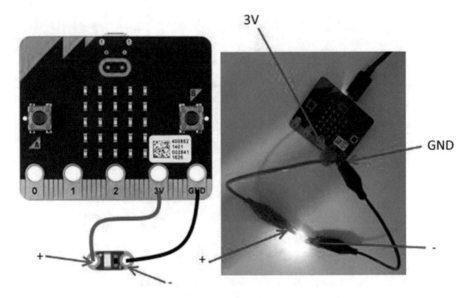

Figure 2-5. *Testing an LED sequin using the micro:bit's 3.3 V power output (left, wiring diagram; right, experiment)*

2.3 Sewing LED Sequins on the LED Textile

The LED sequins should be correctly sewed to the conductive pads on the **LED textile element** to make good electrical contact. If not, they will light at low brightness, flicker, or not light at all.

The only thing you need to sew is the LED sequins that come with the textile kit. We found a great tutorial on how to sew wearable electronics on fabrics at **https://learn.sparkfun.com/tutorials/lilypad-basics-e-sewing/all**.

The Wearic Smart Textiles Kit comes with a spool of conductive threads and a needle. The conductive thread is a polyester yarn that is coated with silver. By following the online tutorial we mentioned previously, sew both LEDs on the LED textile element using conductive threads. When you sew the positive sew tab, the LED sequin should be placed on the positive conductive pad of the LED textile. Also, the negative sew tab of the LED sequin should be placed on the negative conductive pad of the LED textile. After you've sewn both LED sequins on the LED textile, it should look something like Figure 2-6.

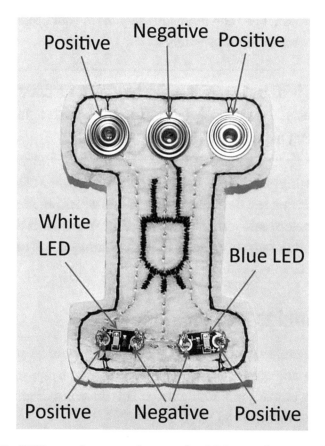

Figure 2-6. *LED sequins sewed on to the LED textile. Note the polarity of the LED sequins: plus on plus, ground on ground*

If you want different colors of LED sequins, search SparkFun (`www.sparkfun.com/`) for **LilyPad LED**. An alternative would be the Adafruit LED sequins (`www.adafruit.com/?q=Adafruit%20LED%20Sequins`).

There are many ways you can power your **LED textile element** with different **powering patterns**. These powering patterns will make different lighting effects such as blinking, flashing, fading, and so forth.

As we have only two LEDs, we can't produce more complex lighting patterns. However, if you add more LED sequins to your project, you can create more complex lighting patterns.

Note   This book only explains to you how to create basic LED lighting effects. You can apply them to make complex lighting patterns using more LEDs.

The following projects will help you understand some of the basic LED lighting effects that can be made with two LEDs which are more useful when you develop real-world e-textile projects. You can mix them with buttons and other sensors to create indicators, and you will learn them in the following chapters of this book.

2.3.1 Blinking and Flashing

In this simple project, you will build a soft circuit and then code it to turn an LED on for one second and then off for one second, repeatedly. That will produce a blinking or flashing effect. This is the basic lighting effect you can get started with an LED.

Both blinking and flashing refer to the on/off alternation but visually different. When an LED is blinking, the on and off are in the same magnitude (in other words, the same delay is used between on and off and off and on). But when an LED is flashing, it emits light at very short intervals; in contrast, the time that it isn't lit is longer.

Your LED textile has two LEDs, but you will use one of them to build this project (you will use both LEDs in the next project to make a flip-flop effect). The circuit is very simple; take the following things to build the soft circuit:

- **micro:bit**

- **Wearic LED textile element** – Has two LED sequins (you will use the blue LED)

- **2 × alligator clip cables** – To connect the micro:bit to the LED textile element

- **3 V battery pack** – To power the micro:bit and the LED textile element

- **Micro USB cable** – To flash the code onto the micro:bit/to power the micro:bit and the LED textile element

Connect the blue LED on the "LED textile element" to the micro:bit using the two alligator cables, as shown in Figure 2-7. Connect the positive pad of the LED to the pin 0 of the micro:bit. Connect the negative pad of the LED to the micro:bit GND.

Figure 2-7. *Attaching the micro:bit to the LED textile element*

Table 2-1 explains how to build the code using **MakeCode** blocks.

Table 2-1. *Step-by-step instructions to build the code for 'blinking and flashing' effect*

Step	Blocks	Description
1		*Use the forever block to build the following code. Every block you place inside the forever block will repeat until you power off/restart the micro:bit.*
2		*Place a digital write block into the forever block. Then change the number to 1. This will send 3.3 V to the micro:bit pin 0 (the blue LED).*
3		*Place a pause block into the forever block after the digital write block. Then select 1 second from the drop-down menu. This will pause the program for 1 second. That means the program will send 3.3 V to pin 0 for 1 second.*

(*continued*)

Table 2-1. (continued)

Step	Blocks	Description
4	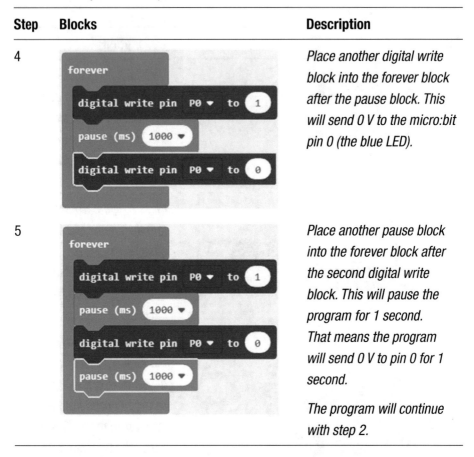	*Place another digital write block into the forever block after the pause block. This will send 0 V to the micro:bit pin 0 (the blue LED).*
5		*Place another pause block into the forever block after the second digital write block. This will pause the program for 1 second. That means the program will send 0 V to pin 0 for 1 second.*
		The program will continue with step 2.

Figure 2-8 shows the full code created using the **MakeCode** blocks. You can also download the shared version of this code onto your editor by visiting **https://makecode.microbit.org/_EUaJMLHUkghw**.

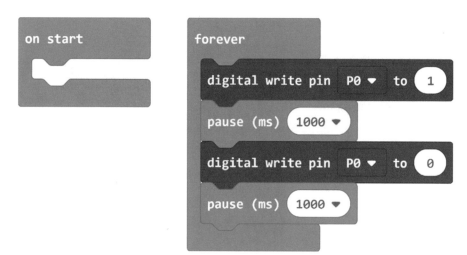

Figure 2-8. *This code makes a blinking LED. The rate of blinking can be changed by editing the time in the pause blocks*

Download the hex file and flash it onto the micro:bit (see **Chapter 1** if you need more help to do that). After the flashing completes, the code will start to run immediately, and you can see the blue LED on the LED textile element starting to blink. Now you can remove the micro:bit from the USB power – your micro:bit will automatically switch to the battery power and continue its function.

Figure 2-9 shows another version of the preceding program that can be used for the **flashing** effect. You can also download the shared version of this code onto your editor by visiting **https://makecode.microbit. org/_4607DHVHbK2V**.

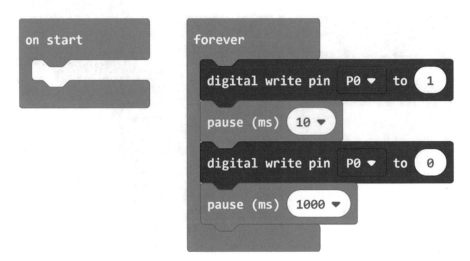

Figure 2-9. *This code makes the flashing effect*

It uses a very small delay (10 milliseconds) between on and off. The time delay between off and on is relatively large (1000 milliseconds). This will make the flashing effect. You can experiment with different time delays to make a good visual effect for flashing.

2.3.2 LED Flip-Flop

In this project, you will use both LEDs to make a flip-flop effect. This will turn on an LED for some time (around 1 second) while turning off the other LED (around 1 second). Then it will turn off the LED that was previously turned on (around 1 second) while turning on the other LED (around 1 second), repeatedly.

For this project, you will need one additional alligator clip cable (we used green color).

Connect the "LED textile element" to the micro:bit using the two alligator cables, as shown in Figure 2-10.

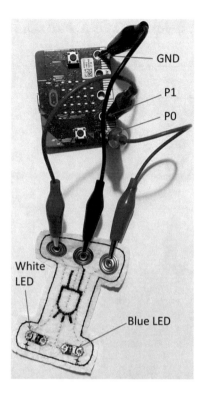

Figure 2-10. *Attaching the micro:bit to the LED textile element. This will connect the blue LED of the LED textile (right) to the micro:bit pin 0 and the white LED of the LED textile (left) to the micro:bit pin 1*

Table 2-2 explains how to build the code using **MakeCode** blocks.

Table 2-2. *Step-by-step instructions to build the code for 'flip-flop' effect*

Step	Blocks	Description
1	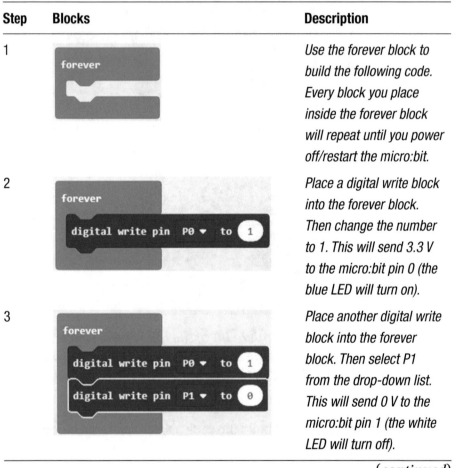	Use the forever block to build the following code. Every block you place inside the forever block will repeat until you power off/restart the micro:bit.
2		Place a digital write block into the forever block. Then change the number to 1. This will send 3.3 V to the micro:bit pin 0 (the blue LED will turn on).
3		Place another digital write block into the forever block. Then select P1 from the drop-down list. This will send 0 V to the micro:bit pin 1 (the white LED will turn off).

(continued)

48

Table 2-2. (*continued*)

Step	Blocks	Description
4		*Place a pause block into the forever block after the second digital write block. Then select 1 second from the drop-down menu. This will pause the program for 1 second. That means the program will send 3.3 V to pin 0 and 0 V to pin 1 for 1 second (the blue LED will turn on for 1 second, while the white LED will turn off for 1 second).*
5		*Place another digital write block into the forever block after the pause block. This will send 0 V to the micro:bit pin 0 (the blue LED will turn off).*

(*continued*)

Table 2-2. (*continued*)

Step	Blocks	Description
6	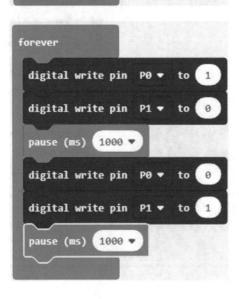	*Place another digital write block into the forever block after the third digital write block. Then select P1 from the drop-down list and change the number to 1. This will send 3.3 V to the micro:bit pin 1 (the white LED will turn on).*
7		*Place another pause block into the forever block after the fourth digital write block. Then select 1 second from the drop-down menu. This will pause the program for 1 second. That means the program will send 0 V to pin 0 and 3.3 V to pin 1 for 1 second (the blue LED will turn off for 1 second, while the white LED will turn on for 1 second).*

Figure 2-11 shows the full code created using the **MakeCode** blocks. You can also download the shared version of this code onto your editor by visiting **https://makecode.microbit.org/_hHfL8p3DcE2w**.

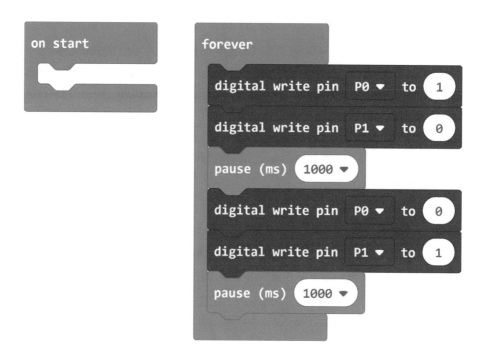

Figure 2-11. *This code makes the flip-flop effect. The speed of the flip-flop effect can be changed by editing the time in the pause blocks*

Download the hex file and flash it onto the micro:bit (see **Chapter 1** if you need more help on how to do that). After the flashing completes, the code will start to run immediately, and you can see the LEDs on the LED textile element starting to blink.

Now you can remove the micro:bit from the USB power – your micro:bit will automatically switch to the battery power and continue its function.

The speed of the flip-flop effect can be changed by editing the time in the **pause** blocks. Make sure to select the same value in both **pause** blocks.

2.3.3 Fading

In this project, you will use an LED to experiment with the fading effect. When starting, the brightness of the LED is at 0 (as if it is turned off). After that, the brightness will gradually increase to its maximum. After it reaches its maximum, the brightness will gradually decrease again to 0. This will repeat continually. The mechanism used to change the brightness of an LED (or speed of a servo motor and others) is known as PWM (Pulse Width Modulation).

Note   Presenting how Pulse Width Modulation works is beyond the scope of this book. However, if you are interested in it, there are many good articles on the Internet that you can read.

Connect the "LED textile element" to the micro:bit using the two alligator cables, as shown in Figure 2-12.

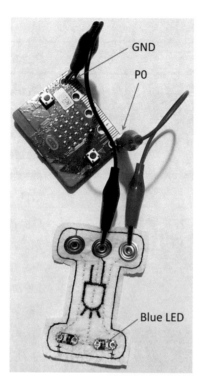

Figure 2-12. *Attaching the micro:bit to the LED textile element. This will connect the blue LED of the LED textile to the micro:bit pin 0*

Table 2-3 explains how to build the code using **MakeCode** blocks.

Table 2-3. *Step-by-step instructions to build the code for 'fading' effect*

Step	Blocks	Description
1	on start	*Use the **on start** block to build the code from steps 2 to 4. Every block you place inside the **on start** block will run only once when you power on/ restart the micro:bit.*

(continued)

Table 2-3. (*continued*)

Step	Blocks	Description
2	set brightness ▾ to 0	Create a variable named **brightness**. Then place the **set brightness** block into the **on start** block. This will set the value of the brightness to **0**.
3	set fadeAmount ▾ to 0	Create a variable named **fadeAmount**. Then place the **set fadeAmount** block into the **on start** block after the **set brightness** block.
4	set fadeAmount ▾ to 5	Then change the **number** to **5**. This will set the size of the **fadeAmount** to **5**.
5	forever	Use the **forever** block to build the code from **steps 5 to 22**. Every block you place inside the **forever** block will repeat after the **on start** block until you power off/restart the micro:bit.
6	analog write pin P0 ▾ to 0	Place the **analog write** block into the **forever** block.
7	analog write pin P0 ▾ to brightness ▾	Replace the number with the variable **brightness**.

(*continued*)

Table 2-3. (*continued*)

Step	Blocks	Description
8	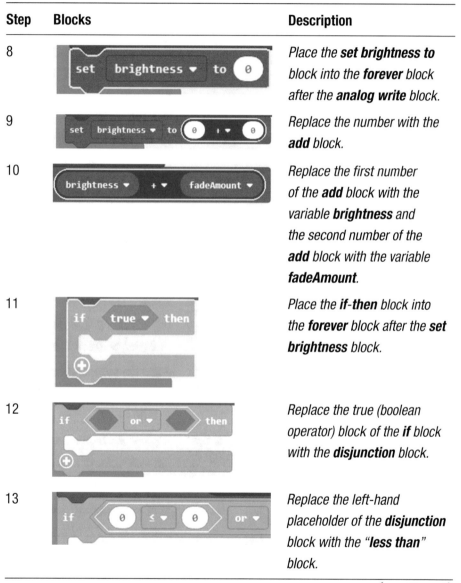	Place the **set brightness to** block into the **forever** block after the **analog write** block.
9		Replace the number with the **add** block.
10		Replace the first number of the **add** block with the variable **brightness** and the second number of the **add** block with the variable **fadeAmount**.
11		Place the **if-then** block into the **forever** block after the **set brightness** block.
12		Replace the true (boolean operator) block of the **if** block with the **disjunction** block.
13		Replace the left-hand placeholder of the **disjunction** block with the "**less than**" block.

(*continued*)

Table 2-3. (*continued*)

Step	Blocks	Description
14		Replace the right-hand placeholder of the disjunction block with the **"greater than or equal to"** block.
15		Replace the left-hand number of the **"less than"** block with the variable **brightness**.
16		Replace the left-hand number of the **"greater than or equal to"** block with the variable **brightness**.
17		Replace the right-hand number of the **"greater than or equal to"** block with **1023**.
18		Place the **set fadeAmount** block into the **then** part of the **if-then** block.
19		Replace the number of the **set fadeAmount** block with a **subtraction** block.
20		Replace the right-hand number of the **"subtraction"** block with the variable **fadeAmount**.

(*continued*)

Table 2-3. (*continued*)

Step	Blocks	Description
21		*Place a **pause** block into the forever block after the **if-then** block.*
22		*Then change the **number** to* ***5.***

Figure 2-13 shows the full code created using the **MakeCode** blocks. You can also download the shared version of this code onto your editor by visiting ***https://makecode.microbit.org/_31jJba6P4AbD***.

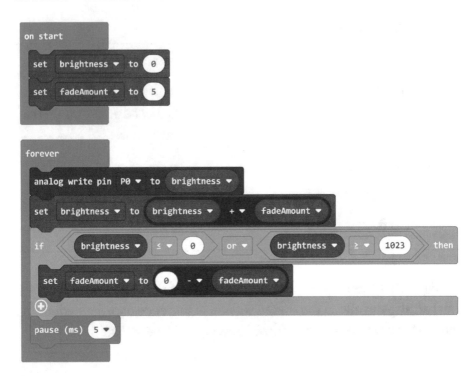

Figure 2-13. *This code makes a fading LED. The speed of the fading effect can be changed by editing the time in the pause block*

Download the hex file and flash it onto the micro:bit (see **Chapter 1** if you need more help on how to do that). After the flashing completes, the code will start to run immediately, and you can see the blue LED on the LED textile element starting to fade.

First, the brightness will increase from 0 (off) to 1023 (maximum brightness) gradually. When the brightness reaches 1023, the brightness will then start to decrease from 1023 to 0 gradually. This will repeat continually.

Now you can remove the micro:bit from the USB power – your micro:bit will automatically switch to the battery power and continue its function.

The speed of the fading can be changed by editing the value in the pause block. The higher the value, the slower the speed of the fading effect.

2.4 Technical Specifications

It would be helpful if you know about the technical specifications of the LED textile element. Table 2-4 presents some of them which are more important when you design a prototype or while attaching the LED textile element to your real garments.

Table 2-4. *Technical specifications of the LED textile element*

Thickness	1.25 mm
Connectors	3 snaps (15 mm s-spring)
Digital output	2 LEDs
Voltage supply	5 V DC
Max. current	50 mA DC
Maximum power	2.5 W
Textile material	Polyester, silver
Protective circuit	Serial resistance
Washability	Limited washability

2.5 Summary

In this chapter, you have learned how to create different lighting effects such as blinking, flashing, flip-flopping, and fading by arranging MakeCode blocks in different orders. You learned how to turn an LED on and off, using delays, loops, simple logics, and simple math throughout the projects. They will also aid you while you go through the following chapter, where you will learn how to use the button textile element (with real soft buttons) with the micro:bit.

CHAPTER 3

Controlling with Buttons

In this chapter, you will learn about how to use the Wearic push-button textile element with your wearables. A push-button textile consists of two soft pushbuttons. By programming the micro:bit, these buttons can be used to control actuators such as LEDs, heating textiles, servos, and so on. The skills you gain in this chapter will help a lot when it comes to following the rest of the chapters in this book.

3.1 The Push-Button Textile Element

Figure 3-1 shows the top view of the push-button textile element. The textile element is made out of a polyester fabric and silver yarns. It has two soft buttons. These buttons are soft and feel like a sponge. Let's label them as buttons A and B so we can easily identify them when you write code for the micro:bit.

© Pradeeka Seneviratne 2020
P. Seneviratne, *Beginning e-Textile Development*,
https://doi.org/10.1007/978-1-4842-6261-0_3

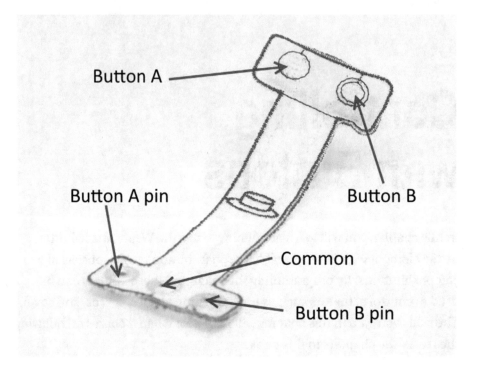

Figure 3-1. *The push-button textile element*

The common snap (pin) on the push-button textile element can be used for both buttons. For example, if you want to connect button A to the micro:bit, you can use the button A pin and the common pin.

3.2 Building the Hardware

The hardware setup (soft circuit) may be a bit different from project to project. However, you will need the following things to build the soft circuits throughout this chapter:

- **micro:bit**

- **Wearic push-button textile element** – Provides two momentary pushbuttons

- **Three alligator cables**

- **2 × AAA battery holder with batteries**

We'll provide the wiring diagrams under each project that you are about to build shortly.

Using a Single Button As an On/Off Switch: Press and Hold to Turn On and then Release to Turn Off

First, let's start with a simple program that detects a button press. This will help you when you want to activate something attached to your garment (e.g., LEDs, servos, heating elements, etc.) by pressing and holding a button. When you release the button, the actuator will turn off. If you want to turn on something manually for a short time, then this is one of the good solutions.

Set up the hardware (soft circuit) as shown in Figure 3-2. Note that **button A** should be connected to the micro:bit **digital pins 1** and **3V**.

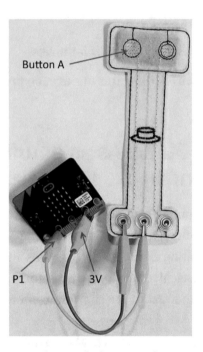

Figure 3-2. *Button A on the push-button element is connected to the micro:bit pins 1 and 3V*

Table 3-1 presents the steps that will help you build the code. The code checks the status of **button A** on the textile button element.

Table 3-1. *Step-by-step instructions to build the code*

Step	Blocks	Description
1		*Use the **forever** block to build the following code. Every block you place inside the **forever** block will repeat until you power off/restart the micro:bit.*
2		*Place an **if-then-else** block into the **forever** block.*
3		*Replace the **true (boolean operator)** block of the **if** part with an **equals (number comparison)** block.*
4		*Replace the left-hand number of the **number comparison** block with a **digital read** block. Then choose **P1** from the drop-down list.*

(*continued*)

Table 3-1. (*continued*)

Step	Blocks	Description
5		Replace the right-hand number (0) of the number comparison block with 1.
6		Place a **show icon** block into the **then** part of the **if-then-else** block. Then choose the **YES** icon from the drop-down list.
7		Place another **show icon** block into the **then** part of the **if-then-else** block. Then choose the **NO** icon from the drop-down list.

Figure 3-3 shows the full code created using **MakeCode** blocks. You can also download the shared version of this code onto your editor by visiting ***https://makecode.microbit.org/_MU0925D3L1uE***.

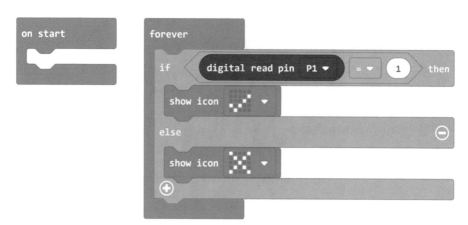

Figure 3-3. *Code to turn on something when pressing and holding a button. Release the button to turn off*

Download and flash the code onto the micro:bit. After completion, the program will immediately start to run and display the **NO** icon on the micro:bit display. That means **button A** is in its **"off"** state. First, press and hold **button A** on the textile button element. The micro:bit display will show the **YES** icon. That means **button A** is in its **"on"** state. Now release the button. The micro:bit will display the **NO** icon again. The program continuously listens to what's happening to button A and displays the button status accordingly.

If you want to control something like LEDs, textile heating elements, or any type of actuator, the hardware setup shown in Figure 3-4 can be used. For example, an LED textile element is connected to the micro:bit as an actuator.

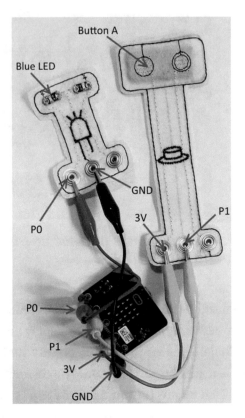

Figure 3-4. *Using a single button to control an LED (Press and Hold to Turn On and then Release to Turn Off)*

Figure 3-5 shows the modified code using MakeCode blocks, which you can use to control the LED textile element. You can also download the shared version of this code onto your editor by visiting ***https://makecode. microbit.org/_AhDbfzbwi5mo***.

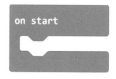

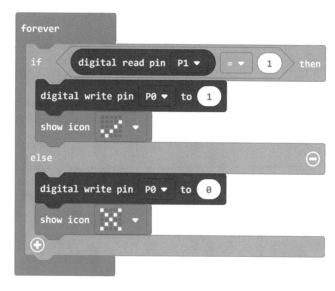

Figure 3-5. *Code to turn on something connected to pin 0 when pressing and holding a button. Release the button to turn off*

Using Both Buttons As an On/Off Switch: Press One Button to Turn On and then Press the Other Button to Turn Off

Now you will use both buttons on the textile button element to control an actuator. As an example, when you press and release **button A**, the actuator will turn on. Then when you press and release **button B**, the actuator will turn off. If you want to turn on something manually for a long time, then this is a good solution.

Build the soft circuit as shown in Figure 3-6. Note that **button A** and **button B** are connected to the micro:bit digital **pins 1** and **2**, respectively. Also, the **common** wire from **button A** and **button B** should be connected to the **3V** pin.

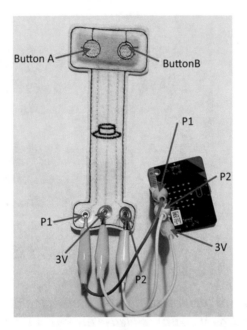

Figure 3-6. *Button A on the push-button element is connected to the micro:bit pin 1, button B to pin 2, and common to 3V*

Table 3-2 explains how to build the code using **MakeCode** blocks. The code checks the status of both buttons on the textile button element.

Table 3-2. *Step-by-step instructions to build the code*

Step	Blocks	Description
1		Use the **forever** block to build the following code. Every block you place inside the **forever** block will repeat until you power off/restart the micro:bit.
2		Place an **if-then** block into the **forever** block.
3		Replace the **true (boolean operator)** block of the **if** part with an **equals (number comparison)** block.
4		Replace the left-hand number of the **number comparison** block with a **digital read** block. Then choose **P1** from the drop-down list.

(continued)

71

Table 3-2. (*continued*)

Step	Blocks	Description
5		Replace the right-hand number (0) of the number comparison block with 1.
6		Place a **show icon** block into the **then** part of the **if-then** block. Then select the YES icon from the drop-down list.
7		Place another **if-then** block into the **forever** block after the first if-then block.
8		Replace the **true (boolean operator)** block of the **if** part with an **equals (number comparison)** block.
9		Replace the left-hand number of the **number comparison** block with a **digital read** block. Then choose **P2** from the drop-down list.

(*continued*)

Table 3-2. (*continued*)

Step	Blocks	Description
10	= ▼ 1 then	*Replace the right-hand number (0) of the number comparison block with 1.*
11	show icon ⬚ ▼ ⊕	*Place a **show icon** block into the **then** part of the **if-then** block. Then select the **NO** icon from the drop-down list*

Figure 3-7 shows the full code created using the **MakeCode** blocks. You can also download the shared version of this code onto your editor by visiting ***https://makecode.microbit.org/_h1jJjoFm323T***.

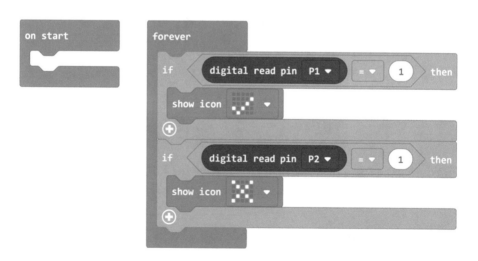

Figure 3-7. *This code checks the status of both buttons A and B*

Now download and flash the code onto the micro:bit. After uploading completes, the code will start to run immediately. When you press and release **button A**, the **YES** icon will show up on the micro:bit LED matrix. When you press and release **button B**, the **NO** icon will display on the micro:bit LED matrix.

If you want to control something like LEDs, textile heating elements, or any type of actuator, the hardware setup shown in Figure 3-8 can be used. For example, an LED textile element is connected to the micro:bit as an actuator.

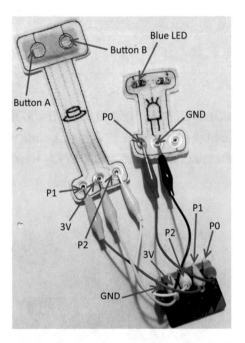

Figure 3-8. *Using both buttons to control an LED (Press One Button to Turn On and then Press the Other Button to Turn Off)*

Figure 3-9 shows the modified code using **MakeCode** blocks, which you can use to control the LED textile element. You can also download the shared version of this code onto your editor by visiting ***https://makecode. microbit.org/_5bLbEz6kz8JL***.

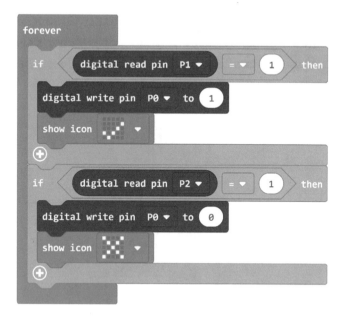

Figure 3-9. *This code checks the status of both buttons A and B and then turns on/off pin 0 accordingly*

Using a Single Button As an On/Off Switch: Press Once to Turn On and then Press Again to Turn Off

In this project, you will program a single button on the push-button textile as an on-off switch. The button will work similarly to the power button on your television's remote control.

For the first time, when you press and release the button, it behaves as an "on" operation of a switch. The second time, when you press and release the button, it behaves as an "off" operation of a switch. Each time, the on/off button toggles between those functions.

First, build the hardware (soft circuit). Connect button A on the push-button textile element to the micro:bit as shown in Figure 3-10. Note that the button should be connected to the micro:bit **pin 1** and **GND** – not to the 3V.

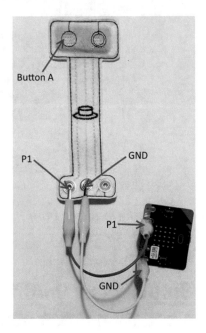

Figure 3-10. *Button A on the push-button element is connected to the micro:bit pin 1 and GND*

Table 3-3 explains how to build the code using **MakeCode** blocks.

Table 3-3. *Step-by-step instructions to build the code*

Step	Blocks	Description
1	on start	Use the **on start** block to build steps 2–3.
2	**Variables** — Make a Variable... — item ▼ — set item ▼ to 0 — change item ▼ by 1	Create a variable named ***item***.
3	on start — set item ▼ to 0	Place the **set item to** block into the **on start** block.
4	on pin P1 ▼ released	Use the **on pin P1 released** block to build steps 5–13.

(continued)

Table 3-3. (*continued*)

Step	Blocks	Description
5		Place the **set item to** block into the **on pin P1 released** block.
6		Replace the number 0 with an **add** block.
7		Replace the left number of the add block with the variable item you created earlier. Then replace the right number of the add block with 1.
8		Place an if-then-else block into the on pin P1 released block after the **set item to** block.
9		Replace the **true** block of the **if-then-else** block with the **equals** (number comparison) block.

(*continued*)

Table 3-3. (*continued*)

Step	Blocks	Description
10		Replace the **left** number of the **equals** block with the **remainder of** block.
11		Replace the **left** number of the **remainder of** block with the variable **item**. Then replace the **right** number of the **remainder of** block with **2**.
12		Place a **show icon** block into the **then** part of the **if-then-else** block. Then select the **NO** icon from the drop-down list.
13		Place a **show icon** block into the **else** part of the **if-then-else** block. Then select the **YES** icon from the drop-down list.

Figure 3-11 shows the full code created using the **MakeCode** blocks. You can also download the shared version of this code onto your editor by visiting ***https://makecode.microbit.org/_3DM1um9F1PKo***.

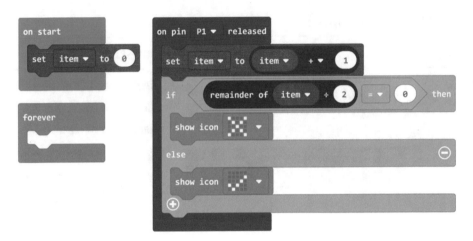

Figure 3-11. *Press button A once to turn on, and then press again to turn off*

Now download and flash the code onto the micro:bit. After uploading completes, the code will start to run immediately. When you press and release **button A**, the **YES** icon will display on the micro:bit LED matrix. When you press and release **button A** again, the **NO** icon will display on the micro:bit LED matrix.

If you want to control something like LEDs, textile heating elements, or any type of actuator, the hardware setup shown in Figure 3-12 can be used. For example, an LED textile element is connected to the micro:bit as an actuator.

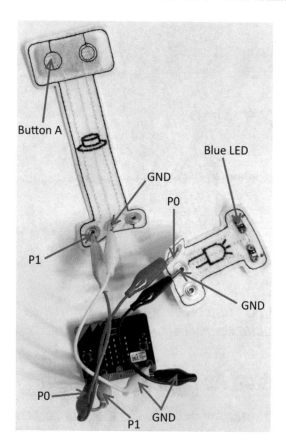

Figure 3-12. *Using a single button to control an LED (Press Once to Turn On and then Press Again to Turn Off)*

Figure 3-13 shows the modified code using **MakeCode** blocks which you can use to control the LED textile element. You can also download the shared version of this code onto your editor by visiting ***https://makecode. microbit.org/_20J9ioXP23sW***.

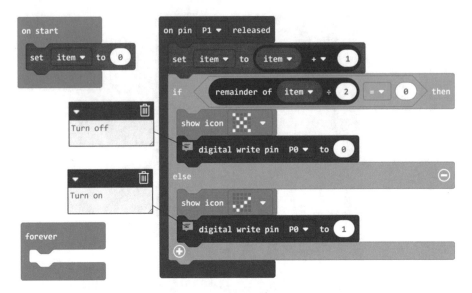

Figure 3-13.   *Press button A once to turn on and then press again to turn off the actuator connected to the micro:bit pin 0*

Using a Button As a Dimmer Switch

Any button can be programmed to work like a dimmer switch. For example, it can be used to light an LED at varying levels of brightness or drive a motor at various speeds. This is known as the **PWM** (Pulse Width Modulation) or **analog write**. The values you can write on a pin range from 0 to 1023. For example, if you want to light an LED at **half brightness,** you can write **512** on the pin where the LED is connected.

Figure 3-14 shows the hardware setup that you can use to control the brightness of the blue LED on the LED textile element. This setup is identical to the setup you built in the previous section.

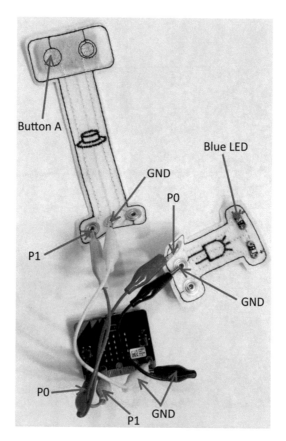

Figure 3-14. *Using a single button as a dimmer switch*

Figure 3-15 shows how to connect two alligator cables to the GND pin on the micro:bit.

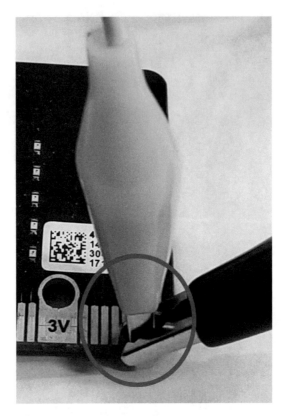

Figure 3-15. *Connecting two alligator clips to the same micro:bit pin*

Table 3-4 explains how to build the code using **MakeCode** blocks.

Table 3-4. *Step-by-step instructions to build the code*

Step	Blocks	Description
1	on start	*Use the **on start** block to build **steps 2–4**.*

(*continued*)

Table 3-4. (*continued*)

Step	Blocks	Description
2		Create two variables named **brightness** and **fadeAmount**.
3		Place the **set brightness to** block into the **on start** block.
4		Place the **set fadeAmount to** block into the **on start** block after the **set brightness to** block. Then replace the number 0 with 100.
5		Use the **on pin P1 released** block to build **steps 6–19**.

(*continued*)

85

Table 3-4. (*continued*)

Step	Blocks	Description
6	analog write pin P0 ▼ to 1023	*Place the **analog write** block into the **on pin P1 released** block.*
7	analog write pin P0 ▼ to brightness ▼	*Replace the number 1023 with the variable **brightness**.*
8	set brightness ▼ to 0	*Place a **set brightness to** block into the **on pin P1 released** block after the **analog write** block.*
9	set brightness ▼ to 0 + ▼ 0	*Replace the number **0** with the **add** block.*
10	brightness ▼ + ▼ fadeAmount ▼	*Replace the left number of the add block with the variable **brightness** and the right number of the add block with the variable **fadeAmount**.*
11	if true ▼ then	*Place an **if-then** block into the **on pin P1 released** block after the **set brightness to** block.*
12	if ◇ or ▼ ◇ then	*Replace the **true** block of the **if-then** block with the **logical or** block.*

(*continued*)

Table 3-4. (*continued*)

Step	Blocks	Description
13		Replace the **left** part of the **or** block with the **less than** block.
14		Replace the **left** number of the **less than** block with the variable **brightness**.
15		Replace the **right** part of the **or** block with the **greater than or equal to** block.
16		Replace the **left** number of the **greater than or equal to** block with the variable **brightness**. Replace the **right** number of the **greater than or equal to** block with **1023**.
17		Place the **set fadeAmount to** block into the **then** part of the **if-then** block.
18		Replace the **0** with a **subtract** block.
19		Replace the right number of the **subtract** block with the variable **fadeAmount**.

Figure 3-16 shows the full code created using the **MakeCode** blocks. You can also download the shared version of this code onto your editor by visiting *https://makecode.microbit.org/_hceL3MLxuOC9*.

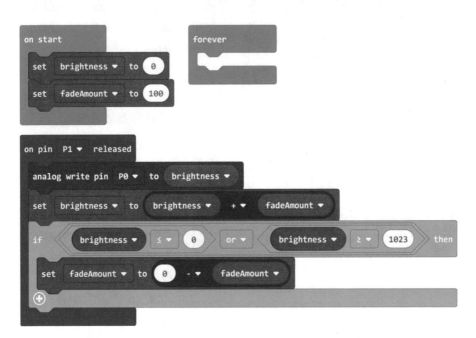

Figure 3-16. *Code for controlling the brightness of an LED by pressing a button*

Now download and flash the code onto the micro:bit. After uploading completes, the code will start immediately to run. Initially, the blue LED won't emit any light.

To fade the LED off and on, gradually increase your PWM value from 0 (all the way off) to 1023 (all the way on) and then back to 0 once again to complete the cycle. In the code you built, the PWM value is set using a variable called **brightness**. Each time you press and release button A, it increases by the value of the variable **fadeAmount**.

If brightness is at either extreme of its value (either 0 or 1023), then **fadeAmount** is changed to its negative. In other words, if **fadeAmount** is **100**, then it is set to **–100**. If it's **–100**, then it's set to **100**. The next time through the loop, this change causes brightness to change direction as well.

If you want to use both buttons on the LED textile element to control the brightness of the LED, build the code shown in Figure 3-17. When you press and release button A, the brightness will increase to its maximum. When you press and release button B, the brightness will decrease to its minimum. You can also download the shared version of this code onto your editor by visiting ***https://makecode.microbit. org/_JC5ftz1XwHsJ***.

Figure 3-17. *Code for controlling the brightness of an LED by pressing both buttons*

The hardware setup you should use with the preceding code is shown in Figure 3-18.

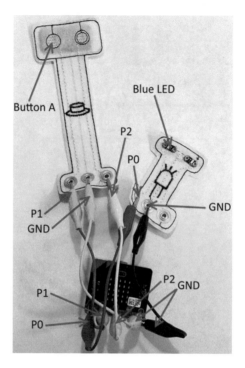

Figure 3-18. *Hardware setup for use in both buttons*

Using the Push-Button Textile Element As a Button Counter

The Wearic push-button textile element can be used to do some action based on how many times the button is pushed. To do this, you need to know when the pushbutton changes state from off to on (or vice versa) and count how many times this change of state happens.

In this project, you learn how to count state changes of a pushbutton and display the result on the micro:bit 5 × 5 LED matrix.

Figure 3-19 shows the soft circuit which uses button A of the push-button element.

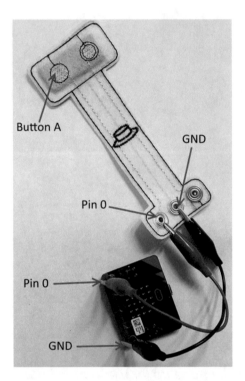

Figure 3-19. *Connecting the push-button element with the micro:bit pin 0*

Table 3-5 explains how to build the code using **MakeCode** blocks.

Table 3-5. *Step-by-step instructions to build the code*

Step	Blocks	Description
1	on start	Use the **on start** block to build **steps 2–4**.
2	☰ **Variables** Make a Variable... count ▼	Create a variable named **count**.
3	on start set count ▼ to 0	Place the **set count to** block into the **on start** block.
4	on start set count ▼ to 1	Replace **0** with **1**.

(*continued*)

Table 3-5. (*continued*)

Step	Blocks	Description
5		Place the **on pin P0 pressed** block onto the **workspace** to build **steps 6–8**.
6		Place the **show number** block into the **on pin P0 pressed** block.
7		Replace **0** with the variable **count**.
8		Place the **change count by 1** block into the **on pin P0 pressed** block.

Figure 3-20 shows the full code created using the **MakeCode** blocks. You can also download the shared version of this code onto your editor by visiting ***https://makecode.microbit.org/_2AJU46C1JDzU***.

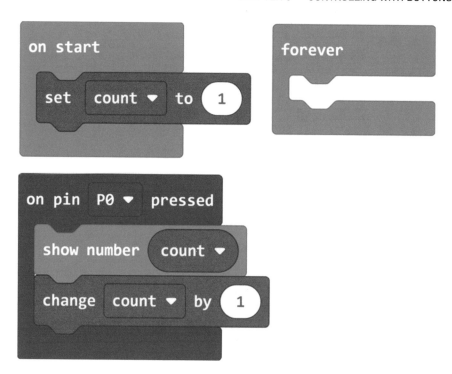

Figure 3-20. *Code for counting the number of button presses*

After building the code, download and flash it onto the micro:bit. After uploading completes, the code will start immediately to run. Now press and release push-button A on the textile push-button element. Each time the micro:bit 5 × 5 LED matrix will display the number of button presses so far.

The preceding code used the state from ***off to on*** to detect a button press. If you want to use ***on to off*** state, just replace the **on pin P0 pressed** with the **on pin P0 released** block.

3.3 Technical Specifications

Table 3-6 presents some important technical specifications that will help you when you make wearable projects with the push-button textile element.

Table 3-6. *Technical specifications of
the push-button textile element*

Size	120 × 50 mm
Digital input	2 pushbuttons
Voltage supply	5 V DC
Max. current	100 mA DC
Textile material	Polyester, silver yarn
Debounce circuit	Low pass
Washability	Limited washability

Caution   Do not use higher current than 100 mA DC and voltage over 5 V.

3.4 Summary

In this chapter, you learned many techniques on how to use buttons on the push-button textile element with your wearable projects. You learned to build code with the MakeCode for each problem as well.

In the next chapter, you will learn how to use the textile heating element for your wearable projects and how to code the textile heating element with the MakeCode blocks.

CHAPTER 4

Staying Warm

In this chapter, we'll use the **Wearic textile heating element** to experiment with heat and then learn how the heat can be applied to wearables to make them warmer.

Living in a region with cold weather can be immensely challenging. You need to wear special types of clothes to prevent the cold from seeping in.

Traditionally, winter clothes helped you stay warm and protected you from the cold. These clothes are made out of synthetic fabrics such as polypropylene, which have several different layers. These layers work as insulators. They prevent body heat from going out through the clothing and keep you warm. However, winter clothes are thicker and heavier and sometimes provide poor insulation. Hence, they aren't comfortable to use for extended periods of time.

So for decades, people have looked into how garments can be heated electrically and electronically (if you needed more control). There are different types of solutions you can find when you search for "heated garments" or "heated textiles" online.

The basic concept behind this is the application of conductive metal yarns/threads into textiles to create electrically heating textiles. It is designed to be a mobile heating solution via the application of DC power sources. These flexible and durable electric conductive yarns can be used for various applications.

© Pradeeka Seneviratne 2020
P. Seneviratne, *Beginning e-Textile Development*,
https://doi.org/10.1007/978-1-4842-6261-0_4

4.1 How Textile Heating Element Works

The **Wearic textile heating element** is made out of stainless steel fibers (a kind of a high-resistance conductive thread) stitched onto a piece of cotton fabric. Then another layer of cotton fabric is added onto it to protect the conductive threads. This is called isolating. Figures 4-1 and 4-2 show how the iron-on technique is applied to **isolate** the bottom fabric layer with another fabric layer.

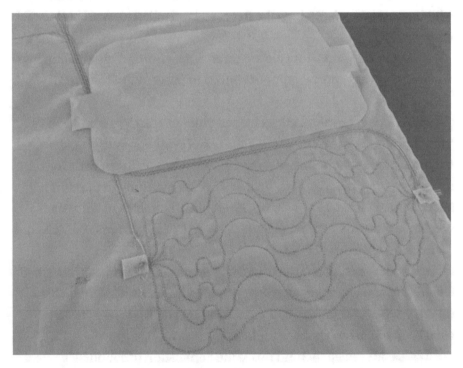

Figure 4-1. *Bottom layer with conductive threads stitched on it*

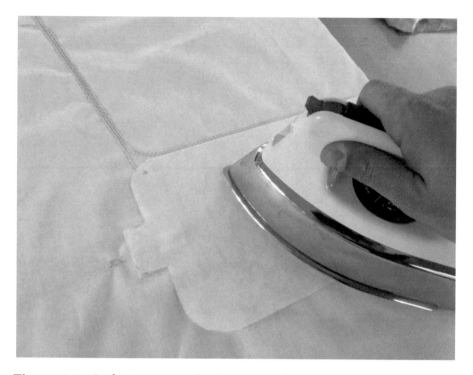

Figure 4-2. *Isolation using the iron-on technique*

These stainless steel fibers have high resistance and produce heat in seconds when you apply power (electricity). The textile heating element is rated at **5 V at 500 mA**. However, you can power it with a 6 V battery pack. Other specifications of the textile heating element are listed at the end of this chapter.

The **textile heating element** has two sides: The **right side** of the textile heating element (Figure 4-3) has the front side of the machine embroidery which presents the heating element symbol so it can be easily identified.

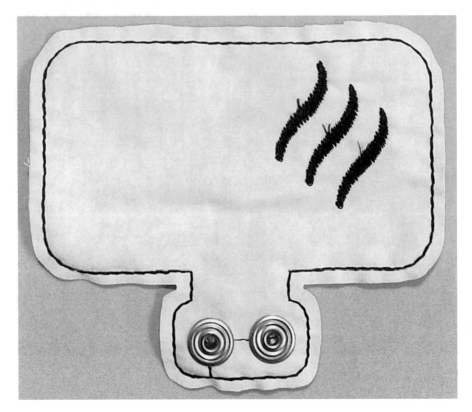

Figure 4-3. *The right side of the textile heating element*

The wrong side of the textile heating element (Figure 4-4) has exposed nonconductive bobbin thread from the embroidery machine. Apart from that, you can see the backside of the machine embroidery which presents the heating element symbol. This can be easily identified by looking at the jump stitches – trailing, extra threads that sometimes appear during machine embroidery.

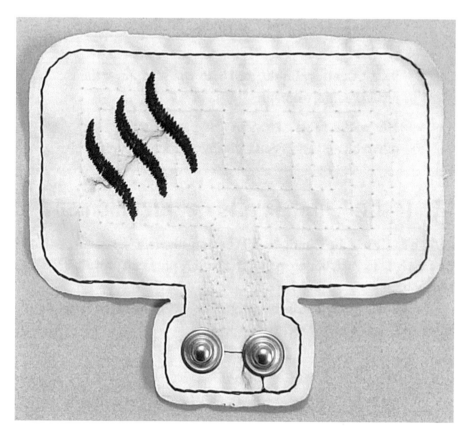

Figure 4-4. *Wrong side of the textile heating element*

There are a few things you will need for nearly all the experiments in this chapter. Here is the list:

- **micro:bit**

- **Wearic textile heating element** – Produces heat when applied power

- **MonkMakes Relay for micro:bit** – Switching high power for the textile heating element and protects your micro:bit (`https://kitronik.co.uk/products/46123-low-voltage-relay-for-microbit-solid-state`)

- **Eight alligator cables** – To connect the things together electrically

- **3 × AAA battery holder and batteries** – To power the textile heating element

- **Micro USB cable** – Provides USB power for the micro:bit and helps you to flash code onto the micro:bit

4.2 Testing Your Textile Heating Element

You can easily test the Wearic "textile heating element" by connecting it to the 4 × AA or 4 × AAA battery pack. The battery pack can provide 6 V with fresh batteries.

Just connect your **"textile heating element"** to the battery pack as shown in Figure 4-5.

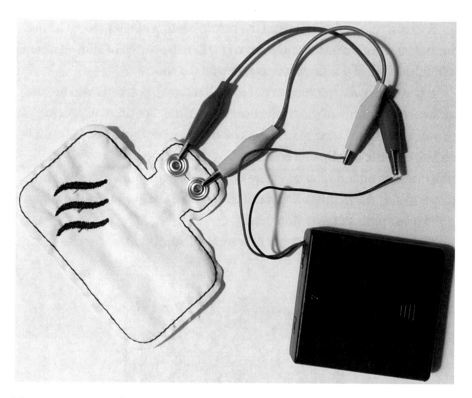

Figure 4-5. *Applying power to the textile heating element using a battery pack*

Note   The textile heating element doesn't have an electrical polarity so you can use either snap with the positive (3V) or negative (GND) wire of the battery pack.

After applying the power, place your palm on the "right side" of the "textile heating element." Within a few seconds, you can feel the textile heating element getting warmer. If you feel too much heat, remove the textile heating element from the battery pack immediately.

A useful rule of thumb is that the textile heating element loses its heat through air conduction. As mentioned earlier, the textile heating element is rated to work at 5 V, but it works fine with 6 V too.

If you have a thermometer (not a medical one), you can measure the surface temperature of the textile during the time. But this will provide you an approximation because the heat will not get evenly distributed on the surface of the textile heated element. The thermometer will report high temperatures on the stitches where the conductive stainless steel fiber goes and also the nearby area of the cotton fabric to the stitches in contrast to the other parts of the cotton fabric.

Figure 4-6 shows a snapshot of the heat distribution we have taken using a thermal camera.

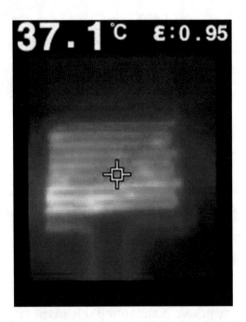

Figure 4-6. *The heat distribution image was taken by a thermal camera. The yellow (middle) indicates a higher temperature than the purple (outer)*

Note   Even if you continually apply power to the textile heating element, it will never become too hot to burn you. This is because the excessive heat gets emitted to the atmosphere.

Supplying the power continually to the "textile heating element" is not a good practice. There are a few other ways you can control the power that goes to the textile heating element. The next few experiments will teach you how to do so.

4.3 Programming the micro:bit

You can use one of the digital pins on the micro:bit to control the textile heating element. There are many ways you can power your textile heating element with different **powering patterns**. The following examples will help you to understand some of them which are more useful when you develop real-world e-textile projects; there could be hundreds of other ways too, but this book only provides you the foundation.

Example 1: Using the Textile Button Element

If you want to control the textile heating element by using buttons, add a Wearic push-button textile to your soft circuit (you learned a lot about how to use pushbuttons with the expansion board in **Chapter 2**).

Connect the textile heating element, the relay board, and the textile push-button element to the micro:bit using alligator cables as explained in the following:

- **Connect the relay board to the micro:bit** – Connect the relay board GND to micro:bit GND and relay board IN to micro:bit pin 0 (Figure 4-7).

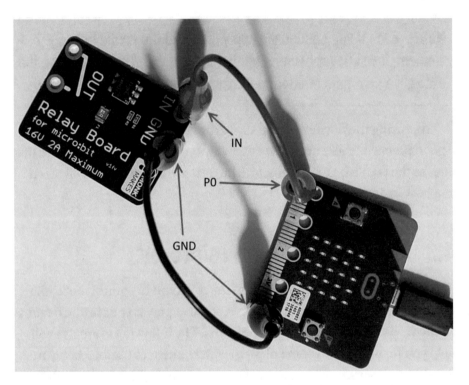

Figure 4-7. *Wiring between the relay board and the micro:bit*

- **Connect the textile heating element and the battery pack to the relay board** – Connect one snap of the textile heating element to one of the pins in the OUT edge. Connect the other snap of the textile heating element to one of the leads from the battery pack. Connect the other lead of the battery pack to the remaining pin in the OUT edge of the relay board (Figure 4-8).

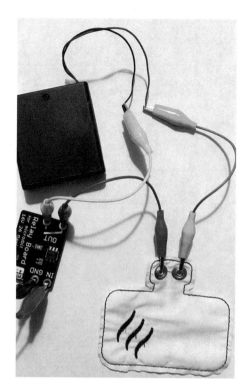

Figure 4-8. *Wiring between the relay board, battery pack, and textile heating element*

- **Connect the textile button element to the micro:bit** – Connect button A between micro:bit pins 1 and 3V. Connect button B between micro:bit pins 2 and 3V. Note that the 3V pin is common for both buttons A and B. See Figure 4-9 to find out which one is button A or B.

107

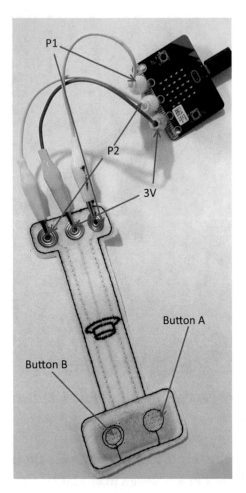

Figure 4-9. *Wiring between the textile button element and the micro:bit*

- Your final setup of the soft circuit should look something like Figure 4-10.

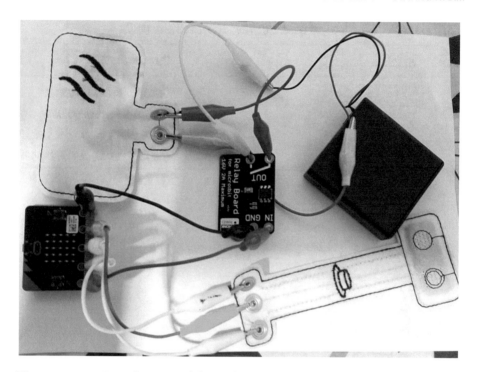

Figure 4-10. *Final setup of the soft circuit*

As the button textile has two buttons, you can control your heated textile using one of the following button control combinations.

Press and Hold Button A to Warm and Release Button A to Cool Down

In this simple project, you will build a soft circuit and then code it to turn on the textile heating element by pressing and holding a button (let's call it button A). When you release the button, the power that goes to the heating element will be cut off. That means it will turn off.

Table 4-1 explains how to build the code using **MakeCode** blocks.

Table 4-1. *Step-by-step instructions to build the code*

Step	Blocks	Description
1		Use the **forever** block to build the following code. Every block you place inside the **forever** block will repeat until you power off/restart the micro:bit.
2		Place an **if-then-else** block into the **forever** block.
3		Replace the **true (boolean operator)** block of the **if** part with an **equals (number comparison)** block.
4		Replace the left-hand number of the **number comparison** block with a **digital read** block. Then choose **P1** from the drop-down list.

(continued)

Table 4-1. (*continued*)

Step	Blocks	Description
5		*Replace the right-hand number (0) of the number comparison block with 1.*
6		*Place a digital write block into the **then** part of the if-then-else block. Then replace the number (0) with 1.*
7		*Place a **show icon** block into the **then** part of the **if-then-else** block after the **digital write** block. Then select the YES icon from the drop-down list.*
8		*Place a **digital write** block into the **else** part of the **if-then-else** block.*
9		*Place a **show icon** block into the **else** part of the **if-then-else** block after the **digital write** block. Then select the **NO** icon from the drop-down list.*

Figure 4-11 shows the full code created using the **MakeCode** blocks. You can also download the shared version of this code onto your editor by visiting **https://makecode.microbit.org/_9bPJtpewK7KP**.

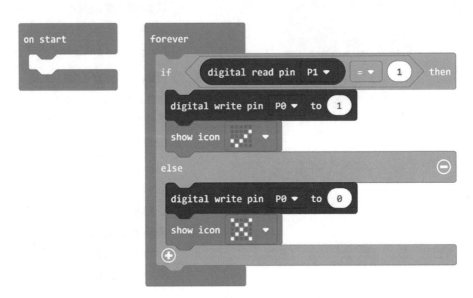

Figure 4-11. *This code checks the status of button A. When you press and hold button A, the heating element will turn on. When you release it, the heating element will turn off*

Now download and flash the code onto the micro:bit. After the upload completes, the code will start to run immediately, and the **NO** icon will display on the micro:bit LED matrix. This means the textile heating element doesn't power up. When you press and hold **button A**, the **YES** icon will display on the micro:bit LED matrix, and the textile heating element will start to get warm gradually. When you release **button A**, the textile heating element will start to cool down again gradually to the normal/room temperature, and the **NO** icon will show up on the micro:bit LED matrix.

Press Button A to Warm and Press Button B to Cool Down

Now you will use both buttons A and B to control the textile heating element. When you press and release button A, the textile heating element will turn on. When you press and release button B, the textile heating element will turn off. So button A works as the on button, and button B works as the off button.

Table 4-2 explains how to build the code using **MakeCode** blocks.

Table 4-2. *Step-by-step instructions to build the code*

Step	Blocks	Description
1		Use the **forever** block to build the following code. Every block you place inside the **forever** block will repeat until you power off/restart the micro:bit.
2		Place an **if-then** block into the **forever** block.
3		Replace the **true (boolean operator)** block of the **if** part with an **equals (number comparison)** block.

(continued)

Table 4-2. (*continued*)

Step	Blocks	Description
4		*Replace the left-hand number of the **number comparison** block with a **digital read** block. Then choose **P1** from the drop-down list.*
5		*Replace the right-hand number (0) of the number comparison block with 1.*
6		*Place a digital write block into the **then** part of the if-then block. Then replace the number (0) with 1.*
7		*Place a **show icon** block into the **then** part of the **if-then** block after the **digital write** block. Then select the YES icon from the drop-down list.*
8		*Place another **if-then** block into the **forever** block after the first if-then block.*

(*continued*)

Table 4-2. (*continued*)

Step	Blocks	Description
9		Replace the **true (boolean operator)** block of the **if** part with an **equals (number comparison)** block.
10		Replace the left-hand number of the **number comparison** block with a **digital read** block. Then choose **P2** from the drop-down list.
11		Replace the right-hand number (0) of the number comparison block with 1.
12		Place a **digital write** block into the **then** part of the **if-then** block.
13		Place a **show icon** block into the **then** part of the **if-then** block after the **digital write** block. Then select the **NO** icon from the drop-down list.

Figure 4-12 shows the full code created using the **MakeCode** blocks. You can also download the shared version of this code onto your editor by visiting **https://makecode.microbit.org/_YcmdMaoC5KxD**.

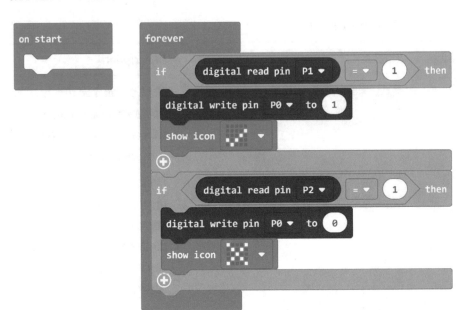

Figure 4-12. *This code checks the statuses of both buttons A and B. When you press button A, the heating element will turn on. When you press button B, the heating element will turn off*

Now download and flash the code onto the micro:bit. After the upload completes, the code will start to run immediately. When you press and release **button A**, the **YES** icon will display on the micro:bit LED matrix, and the textile heating element will start to get warm gradually. When you press and release **button B**, the textile heating element will start to cool down again gradually to the normal/room temperature, and the **NO** icon will show up on the micro:bit LED matrix.

Example 2: Using the micro:bit Temperature Sensor

Your micro:bit has a built-in temperature sensor. With MakeCode, you can read the current temperature known as the ambient temperature. This temperature sensor is located in the micro:bit processor (the Central Processing Unit) and reports the current temperature of the processor. The temperature it reports is closely equivalent to the outside temperature of the processor chip (in other words, the temperature of surrounding air of the processor).

This temperature sensor is very useful when you want to automatically turn on the textile heating element for cold weather. For example, you can program the micro:bit to turn on the textile heating element if the air temperature is below 20 degrees Celsius.

You can use the same soft circuit built in the previous project. Just connect the textile heating element to the micro:bit pin 0.

Figure 4-13 shows the code created using MakeCode blocks. You can also download the shared version of this code onto your editor by visiting **https://makecode.microbit.org/_0h9AFTUpC8DY**. It will turn on the textile heating element if the air temperature goes below 20 degrees Celsius.

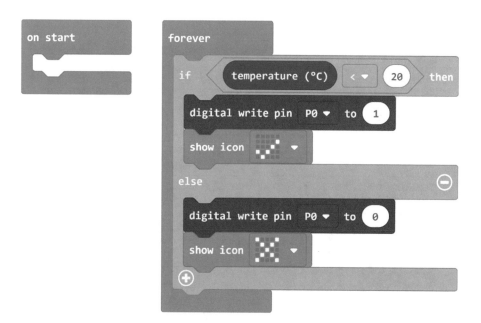

Figure 4-13. *Controlling the textile heating element using the micro:bit built-in temperature sensor*

Once you build the code, download and flash it onto the micro:bit. After the flashing completes, the code will start to run immediately. It will continually check if the air temperature is below 20 degrees Celsius. If the temperature reaches below 20 degrees Celsius, the textile heating element will turn on. Otherwise, it will turn off.

4.4 Applications

Many consumer and industrial applications are using heated textiles. They are widely used in the wearables industry. Other than that, high-temperature heating elements can be applied to build textile-reinforced concrete structures. These structures are implemented in textile-reinforced concrete furniture.

Figure 4-14 shows a textile-reinforced concrete structure, and Figure 4-15 shows a reading of the temperature of the concrete surface using a thermal camera.

Figure 4-14. *Textile-reinforced concrete structure*

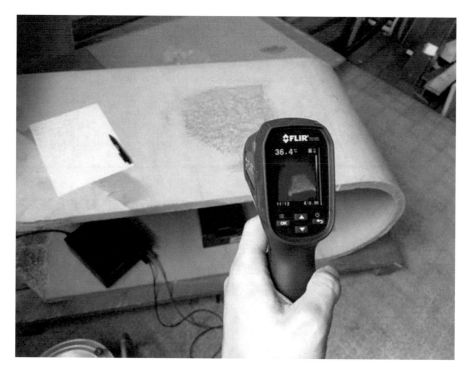

Figure 4-15. *Reading the temperature of a concrete surface using a thermal camera. There is a conductive textile heater in a square shape embedded in the concrete*

4.5 Technical Specifications

It would be helpful if you know about the technical specifications of the textile heating element. Table 4-3 presents some of them which are more important when you design a prototype or while attaching the textile heating element to your real garments.

Table 4-3. *Specifications of the textile heating element*

Size	160 × 90 mm
Thickness	1.25 mm
Connectors	2 snaps (15 mm s-spring)
Heating area	90 × 60 mm
Resistance	10 Ohms
Maximum voltage	6 V
Maximum power	2.5 W
Textile material	Cotton, stainless steel, and silver yarn
Washability	Limited washability

4.6 Summary

In this chapter, you learned to build soft circuits with the Wearic textile heating element. First, you powered the textile heating element using a battery pack. Then you powered and controlled it using the micro:bit and the textile button element. Finally, you controlled it automatically by using the micro:bit's built-in temperature sensor.

In each experiment, you learned how to build code with the MakeCode blocks by snapping different types of blocks together.

There are many ways you can control the textile heating element using the micro:bit that are not covered in this book. Try to control your textile heating element with micro:bit built-in buttons, the accelerometer, and the light sensor.

CHAPTER 5

Textile Pressure Sensor

In this chapter, you will learn how to use the Wearic textile pressure sensor with your wearables to make them pressure sensitive. Textile pressure sensors can be used to detect touch and determine different levels of pressure while squeezing. A microcontroller can be used to read the sensor values and process them to identify the level of pressure or force. The results are used to activate things like LEDs, alarms, and motors or to trigger stuff like text messages, tweets, sending data to IoT clouds, and so on.

5.1 The Wearic Pressure Sensor

The Wearic textile pressure sensor is a type of force-sensitive resistor. It allows you to detect forces such as physical pressure, squeezes, and weight. The pressure sensor is made out of a piece of piezoresistive fabric.

The Wearic textile pressure sensor element is basically a resistor that changes its resistive value depending on how much it is pressed. When there is no pressure, the resistance of the sensor is about 2 kΩ, but at the maximum pressure, the resistance would be about 10 kΩ.

These pressure sensors allow you to design comfortable, lightweight, unobtrusive, and washable wearables.

Figure 5-1 shows the Wearic textile pressure sensor element. The size of the actual sensing area is about 27 × 27 mm, and it feels like a hard piece

© Pradeeka Seneviratne 2020
P. Seneviratne, *Beginning e-Textile Development*,
https://doi.org/10.1007/978-1-4842-6261-0_5

of thin sponge. The far end of the textile element has two "snaps" that you can connect to a microcontroller using alligator cables.

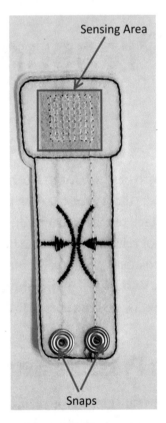

Figure 5-1. *The Wearic textile pressure sensor*

These sensors are easy to use, but they're rarely accurate. The output may vary from sensor to sensor. So basically, when you use textile pressure sensors, you should only expect to get ranges of response. While textile pressure sensors can detect weight, they're a bad choice for detecting the exact number of pounds on them. However, for most touch-sensitive wearable applications, they're a good choice.

The following graph (Figure 5-2) illustrates how resistance changes when a force is applied to roughly assess the characteristics of the sensor.

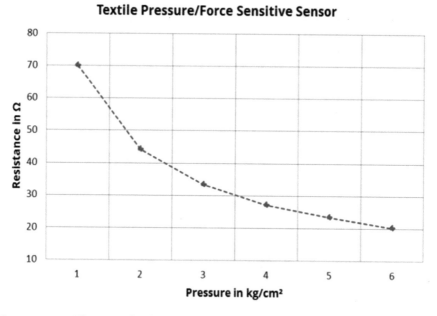

Figure 5-2. *The graph shows how resistance changes when a force is applied to a stamp of 1 cm²*

5.2 Testing Your Pressure Sensor

The easiest way to determine how your textile pressure sensor works is to connect a multimeter in resistance measurement mode to the two snaps on your sensor element and see how the resistance changes by applying different amounts of pressure onto the textile pressure sensor (first start with a soft touch and increase to a big squeeze). Try different ranges with your multimeter, between 20 kΩ and 2 kΩ. Because the resistance changes a lot and you have a multimeter that supports auto-ranging mode at hand, turn it on because an auto-ranging multimeter works well here.

Connect the textile pressure sensor between the **COM** (conventionally black) and **mAVΩ** (conventionally red) probes. Then measure the minimum and maximum resistance of the textile pressure sensor.

5.3 Reading Pressure Values

The easiest way to measure pressure using the textile pressure sensor is to connect its one snap to the micro:bit's 3V pin and the remaining snap to the micro:bit's P1 (you can also use P0 or P2). Then connect a pull-down resistor (10 kiloohms) between micro:bit ground and P1 (the same pin you used to connect the textile pressure sensor). Figure 5-3 shows the hardware setup that you can get help from to build the soft circuit.

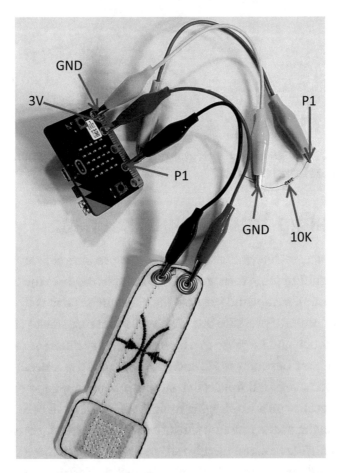

Figure 5-3. *Hardware setup to measure the pressure. Color code for 10 kΩ resistor – brown, black, orange, gold.*

1. Connect one of the snaps on the pressure sensor to the micro:bit pin 1.

2. Connect the other snap on the pressure sensor to the micro:bit 3V.

3. Connect the 10 kΩ resistor between micro:bit pins 1 and GND.

Now you are going to build a code to display the sensor values generated by the textile pressure sensor. The sensor values change rapidly when you apply pressure onto the sensing area of the textile pressure sensor. It is not wise to use the micro:bit 5 × 5 LED matrix to display the sensor values – your micro:bit usually scrolls text and numbers, and it will take some time to display the entire value, so you may miss many sensor readings during the time.

As a solution, you will be writing data on the micro:bit's serial output so you can read them from your computer (as long as your micro:bit is connected to your computer with a USB cable).

The code is very simple. Table 5-1 shows the steps that you can follow to build the code using the MakeCode blocks.

Table 5-1. *Step-by-step instructions to build the code*

Step	MakeCode Blocks	Description
1	forever	*Use the **forever** block. This will repeat everything you place into it.*

(continued)

Table 5-1. (*continued*)

Step	MakeCode Blocks	Description
2	forever serial write number 0	Place the **serial write number** block into the **forever** block.
3	serial write number analog read pin P0 ▼	Replace the number **0** with the **analog read pin** block.
4	analog read pin P1 ▼	Choose **P1** from the drop-down mcnu.
5	serial write line	Place the **serial write line** block into the **forever** block after the **serial write number** block.

Figure 5-4 shows the full code created using the **MakeCode** blocks. You can also download the shared version of this code onto your editor by visiting **https://makecode.microbit.org/_EhagrbirjWqr**.

Figure 5-4. *Code for writing data on the serial port.*

After you complete the code, download and flash it onto the micro:bit. The code will start to run immediately, but you can't see any output on the micro:bit display. To get the values, you should read the micro:bit's serial port.

A **serial terminal program** can be used to read the data on the serial port. We will show you how to use **PuTTY**, a serial terminal emulator on **Windows,** to read the serial port.

Note   The instructions for Mac OS users on how to read the serial output are available at the end of this section.

---

1. Connect the micro:bit to your computer using the micro USB cable.

2. Open Windows **Device Manager** (Figure 5-5). Then, expand the section called "**Ports (COM & LPT)**. Write down the COM port number for **mbed Serial Port** (e.g., COM9).

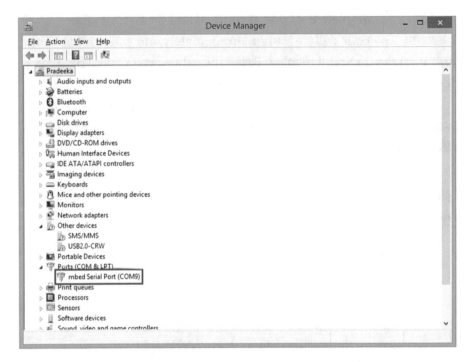

Figure 5-5. *Windows Device Manager.*

3. Download **PuTTY** from *www.chiark.greenend.org. uk/~sgtatham/putty/latest.html*.

4. There are two options (Figure 5-6). The **package files** with the **msi** extension require you to install it on your computer. The **binary files** with the **exe** extension do not require an installation. You can just run the application by double-clicking it. Also, make sure to download the correct version of the file (32-bit or 64-bit) to match your operating system's architecture.

Package files

You probably want one of these. They include versions of all the PuTTY utilities.

(Not sure whether you want the 32-bit or the 64-bit version? Read the FAQ entry.)

MSI ('Windows Installer')			
32-bit:	putty-0.73-installer.msi	(or by FTP)	(signature)
64-bit:	putty-64bit-0.73-installer.msi	(or by FTP)	(signature)

Unix source archive

.tar.gz:	putty-0.73.tar.gz	(or by FTP)	(signature)

Alternative binary files

The installer packages above will provide versions of all of these (except PuTTYtel), but you

(Not sure whether you want the 32-bit or the 64-bit version? Read the FAQ entry.)

putty.exe (the SSH and Telnet client itself)			
32-bit:	putty.exe	(or by FTP)	(signature)
64-bit:	putty.exe	(or by FTP)	(signature)

pscp.exe (an SCP client, i.e. command-line secure file copy)

32-bit:	pscp.exe	(or by FTP)	(signature)

Figure 5-6. *PuTTY package files and binary files download options.*

5. After downloading or installing, start the PuTTY.

6. Use the following settings: **Serial, COM14, 115200**.
   Replace COM14 with the COM port number you
   wrote down previously (Figure 5-7).

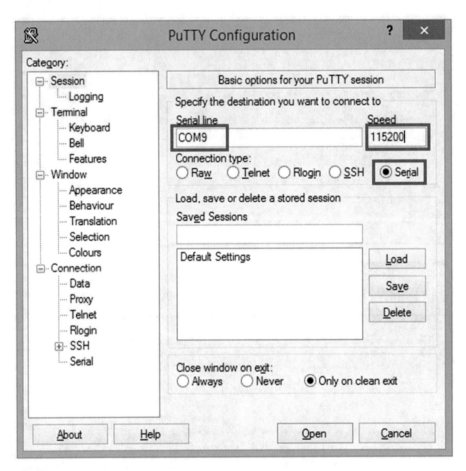

Figure 5-7. *Configuration settings for the Session.*

7. In the **Terminal** section, check **Implicit CR in every LF** (Figure 5-8).

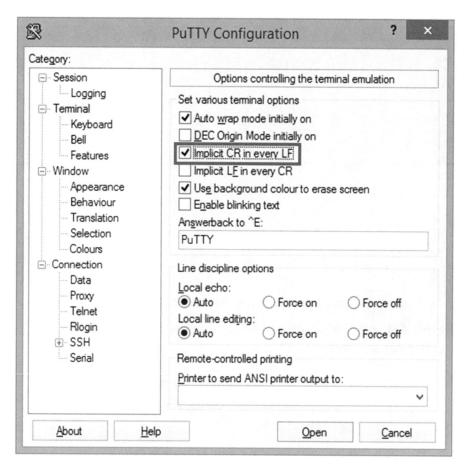

Figure 5-8. *Configuration settings for the Terminal.*

8. Finally, click **Open**.

9. The serial terminal will open, and the pressure
   sensor value will display on it (Figure 5-9).

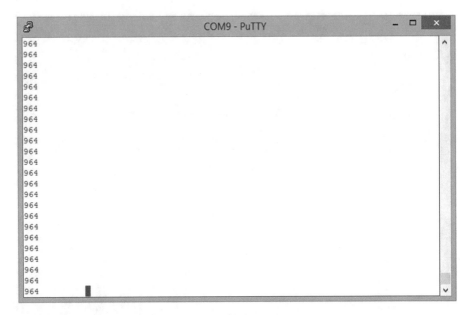

Figure 5-9. *PuTTY terminal without applying pressure onto the textile pressure sensor.*

10. If you haven't applied pressure yet onto the textile pressure sensor, the sensor reading you will get should be at about **964**.

11. Now using your fingertips, apply pressure onto the textile pressure sensor. First, start with a gentle touch and then increase the force. You can see the sensor values increase around **1016** (the maximum you can get is 1023, but you can't practically reach this point) (Figure 5-10).

Note   Not all the Wearic textile pressure sensors produce the same value for the same amount of force. Your textile pressure sensor may produce a different range of values than the values shown in this book.

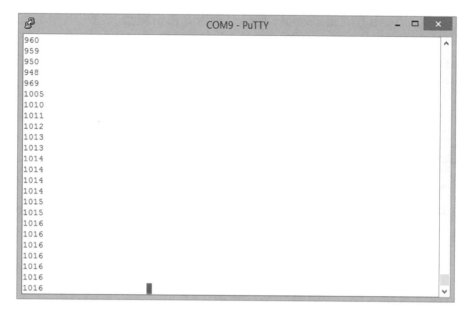

Figure 5-10. PuTTY terminal after applying pressure onto the textile pressure sensor.

This experiment lets you determine the approximate values for different levels of pressure such as light touch, light squeeze, medium squeeze, and big squeeze.

5.3.1 Read the Serial Output in Mac OS

If you are using Mac OS, follow these steps to view the serial output:

1. Connect the micro:bit to your computer.

2. Open a terminal window.

3. Type in **ls /dev/cu.*** and press the Enter key on your keyboard. This will return to you a list of serial devices; one of them will look like **/dev/cu.usbmodem1422** (the exact number depends on your computer).

4. Then type in **screen /dev/cu.usbmodem1422
    115200** and press the Enter key on your keyboard.
    This will open up the micro:bit's serial output.

5. To exit, press Ctrl-A and then Ctrl-D.

5.4 Displaying Different Pressure Levels

In this project, you will display different pressure levels based on the
values you are getting from the textile pressure sensor. Table 5-2 shows the
approximate range of values and pressure levels.

Table 5-2. *Pressure levels
and analog read values*

Values	Pressure Level
0–970	No pressure
970–989	Light touch
990–999	Light squeeze
1000–1009	Medium squeeze
1010–1023	Big squeeze

Note   There is no technical rule or mathematical model to determine
the value range for each pressure level. You can use different value
ranges for each pressure level based on your flavor – remember not
to overlap values.

Now let's build the code to display the pressure levels on the PuTTY terminal when you apply pressure onto the textile pressure sensor. You can use the same soft circuit you built in the previous section (the pressure sensor should be connected to the micro:bit pin 1).

Table 5-3 shows the steps that you should follow to build the code.

Table 5-3. *Step-by-step instructions to build the code*

Step	MakeCode Blocks	Description
1		*Use the **forever** block. This will repeat everything you place into it.*
2		*Create a variable named **pressure**.*
3		*Place the **set pressure to** block into the **forever** block.*
4		*Replace the number **0** with the **analog read pin** block.*
5		*Choose **P1** from the drop-down menu.*

(continued)

Table 5-3. (*continued*)

Step	MakeCode Blocks	Description
6	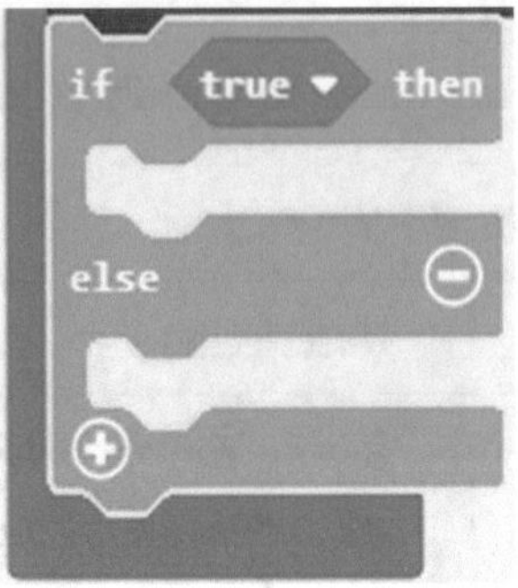	Place an **if-then-else** block into the **forever** block after the **set pressure to** block.
7	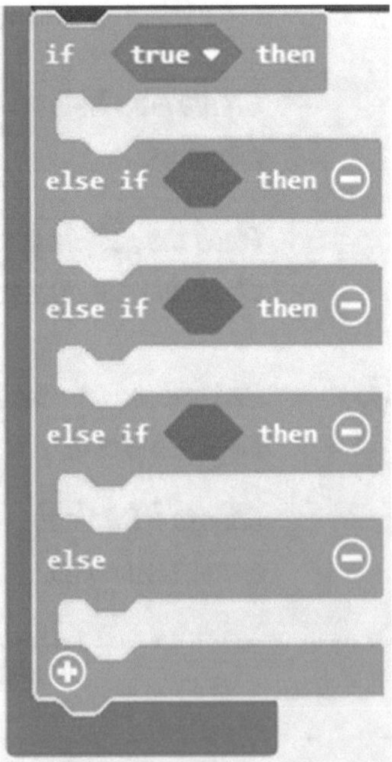	Click **three** times the **plus** button to add three more **else-if** sections.
8		Replace the **true** block with the **less than** block.

(*continued*)

Table 5-3. (*continued*)

Step	MakeCode Blocks	Description
9		Replace the **first input** with the variable block, **pressure**. Also, replace the **second input** with the value **970**.
10		Place a **serial write line** block into the "first" **then** part. Then type in **No pressure**.
11		Duplicate the **less than** block **three times** and place them into the **placeholders** of each of the **else-if** sections.
12		In the "first" **else-if** section, in the **less than** block, replace the **first input** with the variable block **pressure**. Also, replace the **second input** with the value **990**.
13		Place a **serial write line** block into the "second" **then** part. Then type in **light touch**.

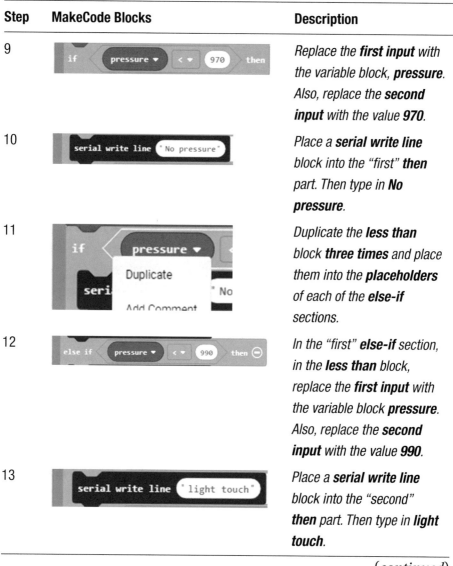

(*continued*)

137

Table 5-3. (continued)

Step	MakeCode Blocks	Description
14	else if (pressure ▼) (< ▼) (1000) then ⊖	*In the "second"* **else-if** *section, in the* **less than** *block, replace the* **first input** *with the variable block,* **pressure**. *Also, replace the* **second input** *with the value* **1000**.
15	serial write line ` light squeeze `	*Place a* **serial write line** *block into the "third"* **then** *part. Then type in* **light squeeze**.
16	else if (pressure ▼) (< ▼) (1010) then ⊖	*In the "third"* **else-if** *section, in the* **less** *block, replace the* **first input** *with the variable block,* **pressure**. *Also, replace the* **second input** *with the value* **1010**.
17	serial write line ` medium squeeze `	*Place a* **serial write line** *block into the "fourth"* **then** *part. Then type in* **medium squeeze**.
18	else serial write line ` big squeeze `	*Place a* **serial write line** *block into the* **else** *part. Then type in* **big squeeze**.

Figure 5-11 shows the full code created using the **MakeCode** blocks. You can also download the shared version of this code onto your editor by visiting **https://makecode.microbit.org/_MUs6KV3gCbdw**.

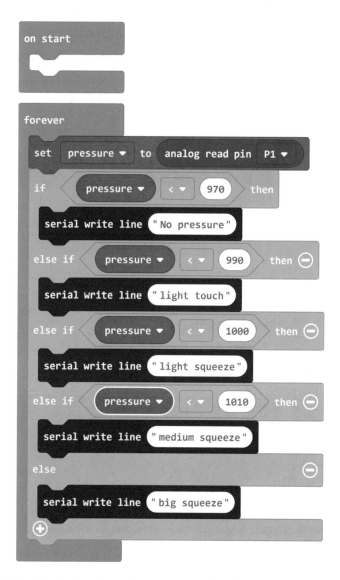

Figure 5-11. *Code for detecting pressure levels.*

After you complete the code, download and flash it onto the micro:bit. After flashing, open your micro:bit's serial port and connect to it using the PuTTY serial terminal emulator. Follow the same steps explained in the previous section to open the serial port. You can use the same serial port unless you have connected any USB devices with your computer after the previous project. However, check your micro:bit's serial port again with the Device Manager.

Similar to the previous project, apply pressure onto the textile pressure sensor using your fingertips. When you increase the pressure, the output changes accordingly as shown in Figure 5-12.

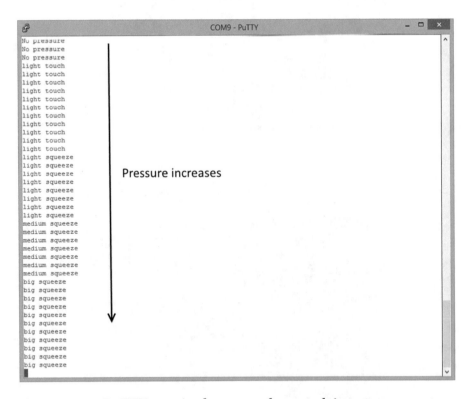

Figure 5-12. *PuTTY terminal output when applying pressure onto the textile pressure sensor.*

5.5 Occupancy Detection

Imagine someone has asked you to build a smart bed. The bed should issue an alarm as soon as an elderly person or child leaves the bed.

As a solution, you can integrate the Wearic textile pressure sensor with your bed. You will need the following things to build the circuit:

- **micro:bit**

- **Wearic textile pressure sensor**

- **MonkMakes speaker for micro:bit** (`www.monkmakes.com/mb_speaker`) – Will amplify the audio output of the micro:bit

- **10 KΩ resistor (brown, black, orange, gold)**

- **7 × alligator cable**

Figure 5-13 shows the hardware setup that you can get help from to connect each hardware using alligator cables. This is just a modification to the circuit you built earlier.

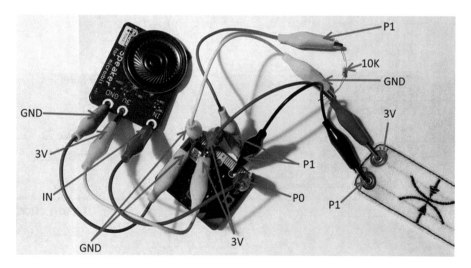

Figure 5-13. *Hardware setup for occupancy detection.*

1. Connect one of the snaps on the pressure sensor to the micro:bit **pin 1**.

2. Connect the other snap on the pressure sensor to the micro:bit **3V**.

3. Connect the **10 KΩ** resistor between micro:bit **pins 1** and **GND**.

4. Connect the speaker **IN** to the micro:bit **pin 0**.

5. Connect the speaker **3V** to the micro:bit **3V**.

6. Connect the speaker **GND** to the micro:bit **GND**.

Now let's build the code. Table 5-4 shows the steps that you can follow to build the code using MakeCode blocks.

Table 5-4. *Step-by-step instructions to build the code*

Step	MakeCode Blocks	Description
1		*Use the **forever** block. This will repeat everything you place into it.*
2		*Create a variable named **pressure**.*
3		*Place the **set pressure to** block into the **forever** block.*

(*continued*)

Table 5-4. (*continued*)

Step	MakeCode Blocks	Description
4		*Replace the number **0** with the **analog read pin** block.*
5		*Choose **P1** from the drop-down menu.*
6		*Place an **if-then-else** block into the **forever** block after the **set pressure to** block.*
7		*Replace the **true** block with the **less than** block.*
8		*Replace the **first input** with the variable block, **pressure**. Also, replace the **second input** with the value **970**.*
9		*Place a **play tone (Middle C)** block into the **then** part of the **if-then-else** block.*

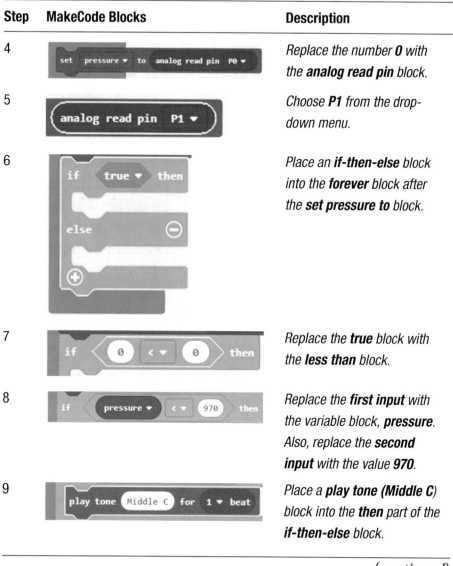

(*continued*)

Table 5-4. (*continued*)

Step	MakeCode Blocks	Description
10		Place a **show icon** block into the **then** part of the **if-then-else** block after the **play tone (Middle C)** block. Then choose **NO** from the drop-down menu.
11		Place a **show icon** block into the **else** part of the **if-then-else** block. Then choose **YES** from the drop-down menu.

Figure 5-14 shows the full code created using the **MakeCode** blocks. You can also download the shared version of this code onto your editor by visiting **https://makecode.microbit.org/_VrYbY1Xz2cRe**.

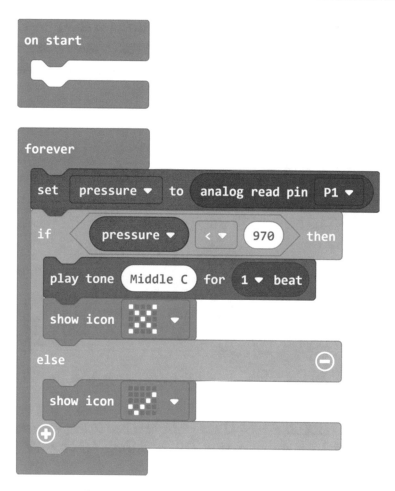

Figure 5-14. *Code for occupancy detection.*

After you complete the code, download and flash it onto the micro:bit. The code will start to run immediately, and the speaker should make a "beeping" sound continually. Now apply some pressure onto the textile pressure sensor. The speaker will stop making the sound.

Most of the occupancy detectors commercially available use the preceding technique to detect the absence of a person. For example, the **TEXIBLE Wisbi** is a bed insert (Figure 5-15) that detects occupancy with the help of a textile pressure sensor. You can read more about the **TEXIBLE Wisbi** by visiting its product page at **www.texible.at/shop/texible-wisbi-pflegeset-classic-betteinlage-sender-steckdoenempfaenger/**.

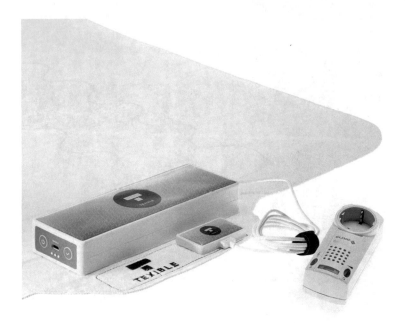

Figure 5-15. *TEXIBLE Wisbi Plus – care set (bed insert, transmitter, socket receiver). Image courtesy of TEXIBLE GmbH (*https://texible.com/*)*

5.6 Applications

Here is a list of common applications of textile pressure sensors:

- Wearables

- Smart homes

- Intelligent workwear

- Occupancy detection

- Weight measurement

- Robotics

- Shoes

- Wearables

- Beds and chairs

- Games

5.7 Technical Specifications

Table 5-5 shows some important technical specifications of the textile pressure sensor element.

Table 5-5. *Technical specifications of the textile pressure sensor*

Size	123 × 48 mm
Thickness	1.25 mm
Connectors	2 snaps (15 mm s-spring)
Sensing area	27 × 27 mm
Resistance range	10–2000 Ohms
Force range	5–200 N
Textile material	Polyester, silver yarn, piezoresistive fabric
Measurement circuit	Voltage divider
Washability	Limited washability

5.8 Summary

In this chapter, you learned how to use the Wearic textile pressure sensor with the micro:bit to detect various pressure levels. In the next chapter, you will learn about the Wearic liquid sensor.

CHAPTER 6

Textile Wetness Sensor

In this chapter, you will learn about how to use the Wearic textile wetness sensor to detect if your garments got wet by liquids such as water and ice.

6.1 Wearic Wetness Sensor

The Wearic wetness sensor can detect small amounts of water or other liquids and ice on its substrate. The most common measurement principle for textile wetness sensors is a resistance measurement between two conductive electrodes. The support fabric on which the electrodes are built is an insulating material (e.g., polyester, cotton, polypropylene).

In the "dry" state, the textile wetness sensor has a very low electrical conductivity. In other words, the resistance is very high at about 1 megaohm. In a "wet" state, the ionic conduction starts, and the resistance changes to 1 kiloohm which leads to high electrical conductivity.

A big advantage of textile sensors is that fabrics absorb and spread liquids very well. Therefore, a small amount of liquid can change the resistance to a large amount. Also, the design of the two electrodes influences very strongly how big the shift is. The smaller the space between the electrodes, the more sensitive the sensor. To minimize noise, it is useful to define a resistance area and adjust a voltage divider for the desired measuring area.

© Pradeeka Seneviratne 2020
P. Seneviratne, *Beginning e-Textile Development*,
https://doi.org/10.1007/978-1-4842-6261-0_6

Figure 6-1 shows the Wearic wetness sensor. The large supporting fabric area detects liquids such as water or ice. The sensor element has two snaps that help you to connect alligator cables. The snaps don't have an electrical polarity, so you can connect them either way with a microcontroller.

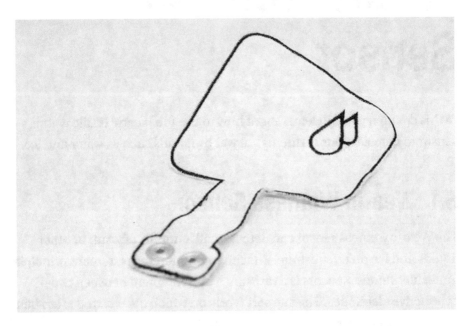

Figure 6-1. *Wearic wetness sensor*

These sensors are easy to use, but they're rarely accurate. The output may vary from sensor to sensor. So basically, when you use textile wetness sensors, you should only expect to get ranges of response. While textile wetness sensors can detect moisture or amount of liquids, they're a bad choice for detecting the exact number of volume on them. However, for most wetness- and moisture-detecting wearable applications, they're a good choice.

6.2 Testing Your Wetness Sensor

The easiest way to determine how your textile wetness sensor works is to connect a multimeter in resistance measurement mode to the two snaps on your sensor element and see how the resistance changes – *the same thing you have done in the previous chapter for the textile pressure sensor.*

- First, measure the resistance of the "dry" textile wetness sensor.

- Then measure the resistance by spraying (you can use a water spray bottle for this) a very small amount of water onto the sensitive area of the textile wetness sensor.

- Finally, measure the resistance by spraying a large amount of water onto the sensitive area of the textile wetness sensor (to make it completely wet).

Try different ranges with your multimeter, between 20 MΩ and 2 kΩ. Because the resistance changes a lot, if you have a multimeter that supports auto-ranging mode at hand, turn it on because an auto-ranging multimeter works well here.

You can perform another experiment using ice. But remember to completely dry your textile wetness sensor before getting started.

6.3 Reading Wetness Sensor Values

The easiest way to measure wetness using the textile wetness sensor is to connect one of its snaps to the micro:bit's 3V pin and the remaining snap to the micro:bit's P1 (you can also use P0 or P2). Then connect a pull-down resistor (10 kΩ) between micro:bit ground and P1 (the same pin you used to connect the textile wetness sensor). Figure 6-2 shows the hardware setup that you can get help from to build the soft circuit.

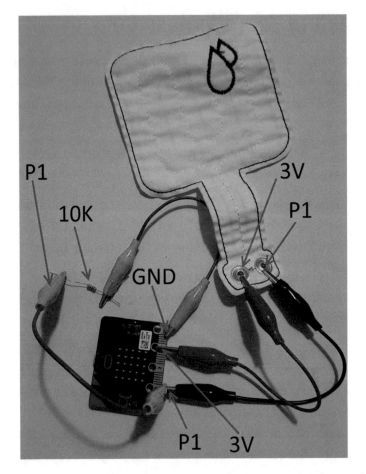

Figure 6-2. *Hardware setup to measure the wetness. Color code for the 10 kΩ resistor – brown, black, orange, gold*

Follow these steps to set it up correctly:

1. Connect one of the snaps on the wetness sensor to the micro:bit pin 1.

2. Connect the remaining snap on the wetness sensor to the micro:bit 3V.

3. Connect the 10 kΩ resistor between micro:bit pins 1 and GND.

Now you are going to build a code to display the sensor values generated by the textile wetness sensor. The sensor values change rapidly when you pour water or some liquids onto the surface of the textile wetness sensor. It is not wise to use the micro:bit 5 × 5 LED matrix to display the sensor values – your micro:bit usually scrolls text and numbers, and it will take some time to display the entire value, so you may miss many sensor readings during the time.

As a solution, you will be writing data on the micro:bit's serial output so you can read them from your computer (as long as your micro:bit is connected to your computer with a USB cable).

The code is very simple. Table 6-1 shows the steps that you can follow to build the code using the MakeCode blocks.

Table 6-1. *Step-by-step instructions to build the code*

Step	MakeCode Blocks	Description
1		Use the **forever** block. This will repeat everything you place into it.
2		Place the **serial write number** block into the **forever** block.
3		Replace the number **0** with the **analog read pin** block.

(continued)

153

Table 6-1. (*continued*)

Step	MakeCode Blocks	Description
4	analog read pin P1 ▼	Choose **P1** from the drop-down menu.
5	serial write line	Place the **serial write line** block into the **forever** block after the **serial write number** block.

Figure 6-3 shows the full code created using the **MakeCode** blocks. You can also download the shared version of this code onto your editor by visiting **https://makecode.microbit.org/_Dw6hC6hPOaet**.

Figure 6-3. *Code for writing data on the serial port*

After you complete the code, download and flash it onto the micro:bit. The code will start to run immediately, but you can't see any output on the micro:bit display. To get the values, you should read the micro:bit's serial port.

In **Chapter 5**, you used the PuTTY serial terminal emulator program to read the micro:bit serial port. In this chapter, you follow the same procedure to read the data coming from the serial port. The following are the same steps you can follow to connect your micro:bit with PuTTY:

1. After downloading or installing, start the PuTTY.

2. Use the following settings: **COM9, 115200, Serial**.
    Replace **COM9** with the correct COM port number
    which has been assigned to your micro:bit (Figure 6-4).

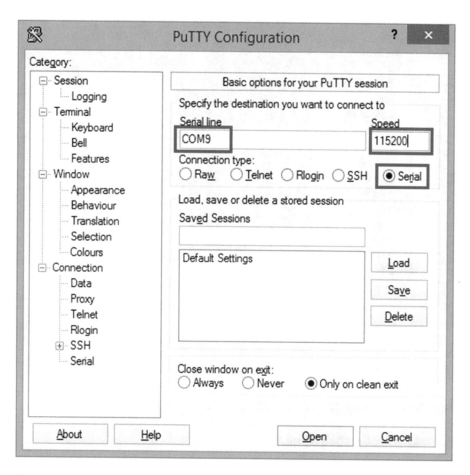

Figure 6-4. *Configuration settings for the Session*

3. In the **Terminal** section, check **Implicit CR in
    every LF** (Figure 6-5).

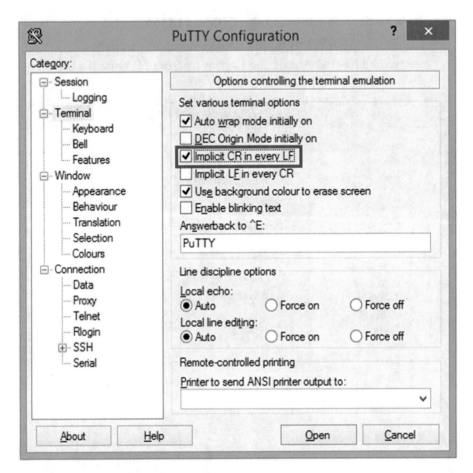

Figure 6-5. *Configuration settings for the Terminal*

4. Finally, click **Open**.

5. The serial terminal will open, and the wetness sensor values will display on it (Figure 6-6).

Figure 6-6. *PuTTY terminal output, without pouring water/placing ice onto the textile wetness sensor*

6.   If you haven't poured water or added ice yet onto the textile wetness sensor, the sensor reading you will get should be at about **9**.

7.   Now pour water onto the textile wetness sensor. First, start with a small amount of water and then increase the amount of water to make the sensor fully wet. You can see the sensor values increase to around **370** (the maximum you can get is 1023, but you can't practically reach this point) (Figure 6-7).

Note   Not all the Wearic textile wetness sensors produce the same value for the same amount of water. Your textile wetness sensor may produce a different range of values than the values shown in this book.

Figure 6-7. *PuTTY terminal output after pouring a large amount of water onto the textile wetness sensor*

This experiment lets you determine the approximate values for different amounts of water and ice (or you can experiment with other liquids too).

6.3.1 Read the Serial Output in Mac OS

If you are using Mac OS, follow these steps to view the serial output:

1. Connect the micro:bit to your computer.

2. Open a terminal window.

3. Type **ls /dev/cu.*** and press the Enter key on the keyboard.

   This will return to you a list of serial devices; one of them will look like **/dev/cu.usbmodem1422** (the exact number depends on your computer).

4. Type **screen /dev/cu.usbmodem1422 115200** and press the Enter key on the keyboard.

    This will open up the micro:bit's serial output.

5. To exit, press **Ctrl-A** followed by **Ctrl-D**.

6.4 Displaying Different Wetness Levels

In this project, you will display different wetness levels based on the values you are getting from the textile wetness sensor. Table 6-2 shows the approximate range of values and wetness levels.

Table 6-2. *Wetness levels and analog read values*

Values	Wetness Level
0–9	Dry
10–150	Slightly wet
151–250	Medium wet
251–1023	Fully wet

Note   There is no technical rule or mathematical model to determine the value range for each wetness level. You can use different value ranges for each wetness level based on your requirement – but remember not to overlap values.

Now let's build the code to display the wetness levels on the PuTTY terminal when you apply different amounts of liquid onto the textile wetness sensor. You can use the same soft circuit you built in the previous section (the wetness sensor should be connected to the micro:bit pin 1).

Table 6-3 shows the steps that you should follow to build the code.

Table 6-3. *Step-by-step instructions to build the code*

Step	MakeCode Blocks	Description
1		Use the **forever** block. This will repeat everything you place into it.
2		Create a variable named **wetness**.
3		Place the **set wetness to** block into the **forever** block.
4		Replace the number **0** with the **analog read pin** block.
5		Choose **P1** from the drop-down menu.
6		Place an **if-then-else** block into the **forever** block after the **set wetness to** block.

(*continued*)

Table 6-3. (*continued*)

Step	MakeCode Blocks	Description
7		Click two times the **plus** button to add two more **else-if** sections.
8		Replace the **true** block with the **less than** block.
9		Replace the **first input** with the variable block, **wetness**. Also, replace the **second input** with the value **10**.
10		Place a **serial write line** block into the "first" **then** part. Then type in **dry**.

(*continued*)

Table 6-3. (*continued*)

Step	MakeCode Blocks	Description
11		Duplicate the **less than** block **two times** and place them into the **placeholders** of each of the **else-if** sections.
12		In the "first" **else-if** section, in the **less than** block, replace the **first input** with the variable block **wetness**. Also, replace the **second input** with the value **151**.
13		Place a **serial write line** block into the "second" **then** part. Then type in **slightly wet**.
14		In the "second" **else-if** section, in the **less than** block, replace the **first input** with the variable block, **wetness**. Also, replace the **second input** with the value **251**.
15		Place a **serial write line** block into the "third" **then** part. Then type in **medium wet**.
16		Place a **serial write line** block into the **else** part. Then type in **fully wet**.

Figure 6-8 shows the full code created using the **MakeCode** blocks. You can also download the shared version of this code onto your editor by visiting **https://makecode.microbit.org/_9efKy7KuFAAp**.

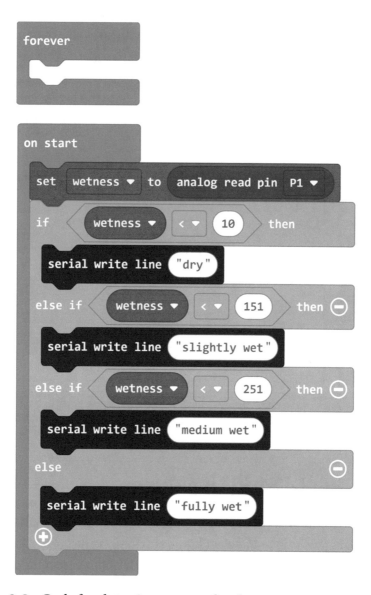

Figure 6-8. *Code for detecting wetness levels*

After you complete the code, download and flash it onto the micro:bit. After flashing, open your micro:bit's serial port and connect to it using the PuTTY serial terminal emulator. Follow the same steps explained in the previous section to open the serial port. You can use the same serial port unless you have connected any USB devices with your computer after the previous project. However, check your micro:bit's serial port again with the Device Manager.

Similar to the previous project, pour water onto the textile wetness sensor. When you increase the amount of water, the output changes accordingly as shown in Figure 6-9.

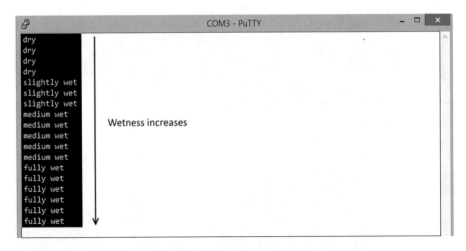

Figure 6-9. *PuTTY terminal output when pouring water onto the textile wetness sensor*

6.5 A Real-World Use Case

Most of the wetness detectors commercially available in the market use the preceding technique to detect liquids on their surface. For example, The **TEXIBLE Wisbi** bed insert (Figure 6-10) detects wetness for people who suffer from urinary incontinence. If wetness from the bed is detected, a notification is automatically sent to the app or the recipient. A delay can also be set as required.

You can read more about the TEXIBLE Wisbi by visiting its product page at **www.texible.at/shop/texible-wisbi-pflegeset-classic-betteinlage-sender-steckdoenempfaenger/**.

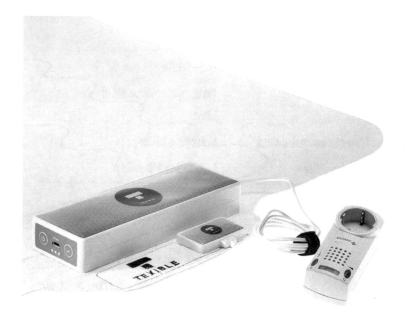

Figure 6-10. *TEXIBLE Wisbi Plus – care set (bed insert, transmitter, socket receiver). Image courtesy of TEXIBLE GmbH (*`https://texible.com/`*)*

6.6 Technical Specifications

Table 6-4 shows some important technical specifications of the textile wetness sensor element.

Table 6-4. *Technical specifications of the textile wetness sensor*

Size	180 × 90 mm
Thickness	1.25 mm
Connectors	2 snaps (15 mm s-spring)
Sensing area	100 × 100 mm
Resistance range	1 kΩ–1 MΩ
Liquid amount	0.5–10 ml
Textile material	Cotton, stainless steel yarn
Measurement circuit	Voltage divider
Washability	Limited washability

6.7 Summary

In this chapter, you learned how to use the Wearic textile wetness sensor with the micro:bit to detect various wetness levels. In the next chapter, you will learn how to send the textile sensor data to a smartphone (or tablet) using Bluetooth Low Energy.

CHAPTER 7

Sending Sensor Data Using Bluetooth

Throughout the previous chapters, you used micro:bit to code textile elements. The Wearic Smart Textiles Kit doesn't include any textile elements to enable wireless connectivity. Fortunately, the micro:bit has a built-in Bluetooth Low Energy (BLE) radio for short-range wireless communication.

The Bluetooth Low Energy provides short-range wireless connectivity that is location-aware and context-aware. It allows you to send and receive small data packets between the micro:bit (or any other microcontroller) and a "connected" Bluetooth Low Energy central device on the other end such as a smartphone or tablet running the Adafruit Bluefruit LE Connect app on Android or iOS. The Bluetooth Low Energy radio can send small data packets to the connected app using Universal Asynchronous Receiver-Transmitter (UART) over Bluetooth Low Energy.

Bluetooth Low Energy–based communication is an efficient, energy-saving option for building IoT applications in categories such as home automation, healthcare, retail mobile tracking, and security. So you can use battery power to run your micro:bit for months (unless you use the LED display). It is possible to use Bluetooth Low Energy without pairing your micro:bit with your smartphone or tablet.

© Pradeeka Seneviratne 2020
P. Seneviratne, *Beginning e-Textile Development*,
https://doi.org/10.1007/978-1-4842-6261-0_7

In this chapter, first, you will learn how to apply the Bluetooth Low Energy feature on your micro:bit to send Wearic textile pressure sensor data to an app running on your smartphone or tablet. Then you will learn how to control your mobile device with the micro:bit using Bluetooth Low energy. Both will be fun and exciting projects!

7.1 Building the Bluetooth Pressure Sensor

You already know that the main chip of the micro:bit has Bluetooth Low Energy radio built in, so you don't need additional hardware to add the Bluetooth Low Energy feature.

You will need the following things to build the Bluetooth pressure sensor:

- **micro:bit** – Provides a microprocessor and a Bluetooth radio

- **2 × AAA battery pack** – Powers your micro:bit after removing the micro USB cable from the computer

- **Micro USB cable** – Allows you to flash code onto the micro:bit

- **Wearic textile pressure sensor** – Works as the sensor

- **10 KΩ resistor** – Helps to pull down pin 1

- **Alligator leads** – To connect things together

Our Bluetooth textile pressure sensor is very simple. Connect the components as shown in Figure 7-1. Use the micro:bit **pin 1** to connect the pressure sensor.

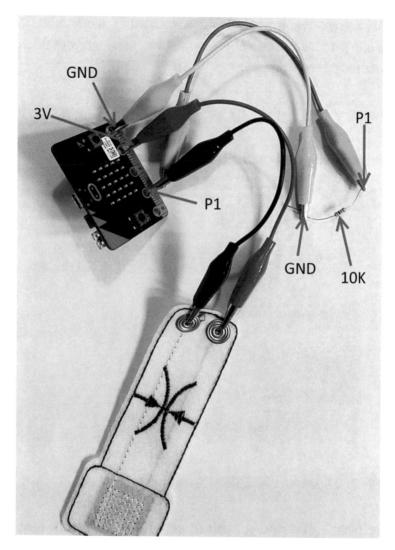

Figure 7-1. *Connecting the micro:bit with the textile pressure sensor*

In addition to that, you will need a smartphone or tablet running Android or iOS with an Internet connection (cellular or WiFi).

Go to **Google Play** and install the **micro:bit UART Terminal** app (`https://play.google.com/store/apps/details?id=com.ble.microbit.uart&hl=en`) on your smartphone or tablet (Figure 7-2).

There are many other apps available to work with the micro:bit UART, but this app provides more stable connectivity between your micro:bit and the smartphone or tablet.

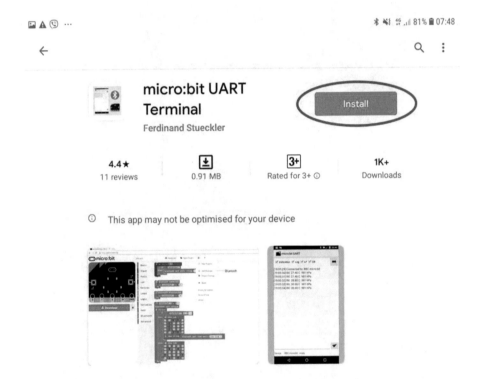

Figure 7-2. The micro:bit UART Terminal app

After installing the app, you can access it from your mobile device's home screen (Figure 7-3).

Figure 7-3. *micro:bit UART Terminal app shortcut icon on the home screen*

7.2 Preparing the Development Environment

To write the code, we will choose the **Bluetooth** extension that comes with the MakeCode. Follow these steps to add it to your MakeCode project:

- Click the **cogwheel** button at the top-right corner in your MakeCode project window. Then from the drop-down menu, click **Extensions** (Figure 7-4).

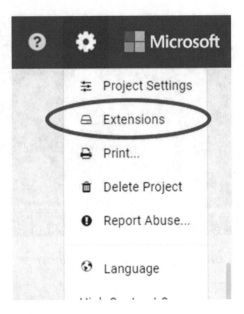

Figure 7-4. *MakeCode Extensions menu*

- In the Extensions page, choose **Bluetooth**. If you can't see it, just search using the term "**Bluetooth**." It will appear on the page (Figure 7-5).

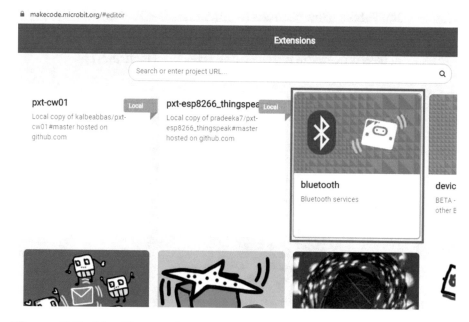

Figure 7-5. *The Bluetooth extension*

- Click the **Remove extension(s) and add bluetooth**
  button (Figure 7-6). This is a mandatory step. You can't
  keep both the radio and Bluetooth extensions together
  because they will make conflicts.

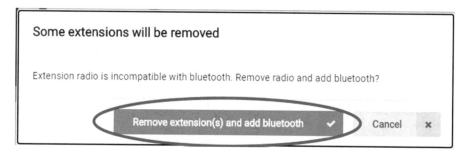

Figure 7-6. *Removing the radio extension*

- It will take a few seconds to download the Bluetooth extension to your MakeCode project, and you can access it from the **blocks categories** box (Figure 7-7).

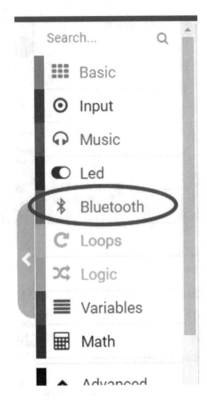

Figure 7-7.   The Bluetooth extension

7.3 Coding the Bluetooth Textile Pressure Sensor

Now you have set up all the things that you require to write the code and run the project. Follow the steps in Table 7-1 to build the code step by step with the MakeCode editor. You can also use the full code listing at the end of this section, or you can download the pre-compiled code (the hex file) from the book's GitHub repository.

Table 7-1. *Step-by-step instructions to build the code*

Step	MakeCode Blocks	Description
1	on start — bluetooth uart service	Place the **bluetooth uart service** block into the **on start** block.
2	on bluetooth connected	Place the **on bluetooth connected** block onto the editor.
3	on bluetooth connected — show icon	Place the **show icon** block into the **on bluetooth connected** block. Then choose the **YES** icon from the drop-down list.
4	on bluetooth disconnected	Place the **on bluetooth disconnected** block onto the editor.
5	on bluetooth disconnected — show icon	Place the **show icon** block into the **on bluetooth disconnected** block. Then choose the **NO** icon from the drop-down list.

(continued)

175

Table 7-1. (*continued*)

Step	MakeCode Blocks	Description
6		Use the **forever** block. This will repeat everything you place into it.
7		Place the **bluetooth uart write number** block into the **forever** block.
8		Place **analog read pin** block into the **bluetooth uart write number** block. Then select **P1** from the drop-down list.
9		Place **pause (ms)** block into the **forever** block and then select **1 second** from the drop-down list. This tells the micro:bit to send data every 1 second.

Figure 7-8 shows the full code created using the **MakeCode** blocks. You can also download the shared version of this code onto your editor by visiting **https://makecode.microbit.org/_FvvgDp9mL85J**.

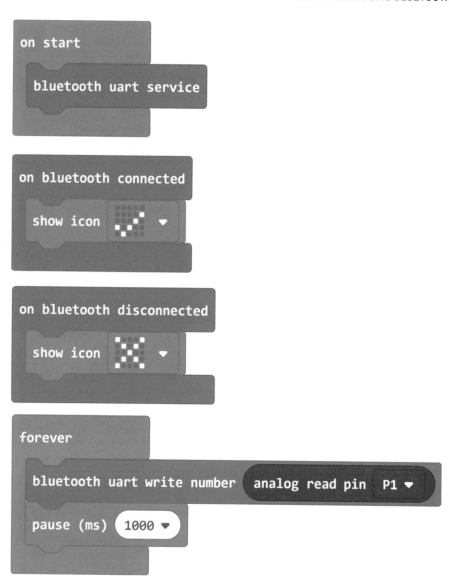

Figure 7-8. *Code for sending data through the Bluetooth UART*

That's all. Now you're ready to flash the code onto the micro:bit. The following steps will guide you on how to do that:

- First, connect the micro:bit with your computer using the micro USB cable.

- Then click the **Download** button to download the hex file onto your computer. Then drag and drop it onto the micro:bit drive.

7.4 Displaying Data

Now you are ready to view sensor data with your smartphone or tablet. The following steps explain how to do that:

- Turn on Bluetooth (Figure 7-9) on your mobile device.

Figure 7-9. *Bluetooth connectivity is on*

- Open the micro:bit UART Terminal app.

- **Allow micro:bit UART** to access your device's location (Figure 7-10).

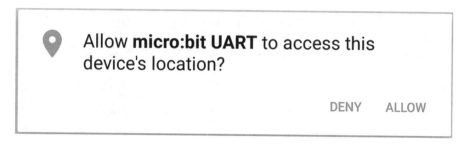

Figure 7-10. *Allow the micro:bit UART app to access the device's location*

- Click the **"double-arrow"** button in the top-right corner of the screen (Figure 7-11).

Figure 7-11. *The "double-arrow" button will open the scan window*

- Within a few seconds, the name of your micro:bit will display on the screen. Just select it to connect to your micro:bit (Figure 7-12).

Figure 7-12.   Selecting the micro:bit.

- When your micro:bit is connected with the mobile device (smartphone or tablet), the **YES** icon will display on the micro:bit 5 × 5 LED matrix.

- The terminal window will open and display the sensor data (Figure 7-13). You can apply some pressure on the pressure sensor to see how the values get changed.

Figure 7-13. *The terminal window displays sensor data*

7.5 Other Apps for Sending Sensor Data

The **micro:bit UART Terminal** app allows you to send sensor data to a mobile device. However, some apps allow sending data to IoT clouds but don't work with the MakeCode. As an example, the **Adafruit Bluefruit LE Connect** app allows sending data to the Adafruit IO using the MQTT protocol. Unfortunately, it doesn't support micro:bit code written in MakeCode blocks.

Bitty Blue is another app you can use to send sensor data to your mobile device. You can download it onto your Android mobile device from the **Google Play Store** (`https://play.google.com/store/apps/details?id=com.bittysoftware.bittyblue.BittyBlue&hl=en`) (Figure 7-14).

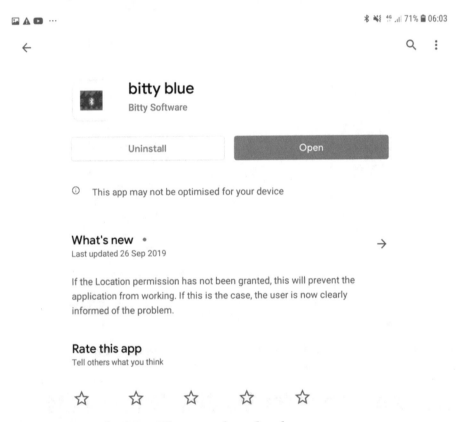

Figure 7-14. *The Bitty Blue app download page*

The following steps will guide you on how to view data with the Bitty Blue:

- Open the Bitty Blue app.

- Select **Scan**. Within a few seconds, the name (also the id) of your micro:bit will display in the list. Just select it to connect to your micro:bit (Figure 7-15).

Figure 7-15. *List of available micro:bits with Bluetooth enabled*

- In the **Bitty Blue – Menu** screen, select **Message Display** (Figure 7-16).

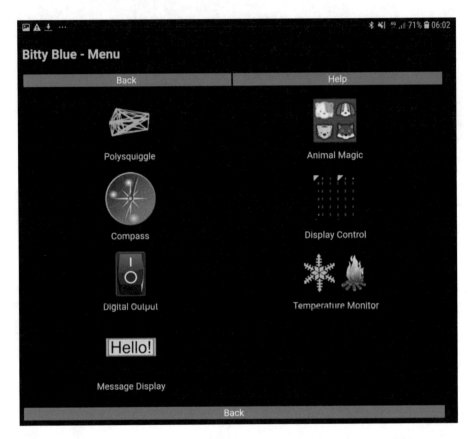

Figure 7-16. *Bitty Blue menu which allows you to choose different options*

- In the **Message Display** screen, you can see the sensor data coming from the micro:bit (Figure 7-17). You can apply pressure onto the pressure sensor to see how the values get changed.

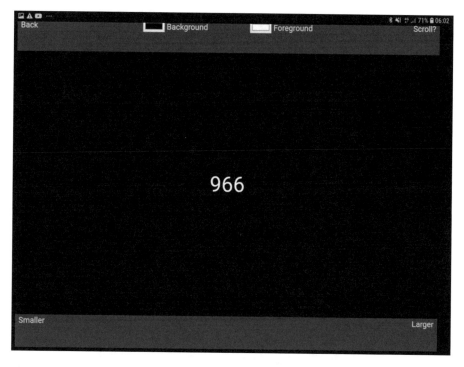

Figure 7-17. *Bitty Blue displays textile pressure sensor data*

7.6 Controlling Your Phone: Wearable Selfie Button

With the micro:bit, you can control your phone using the **official micro:bit app** (Figure 7-18).

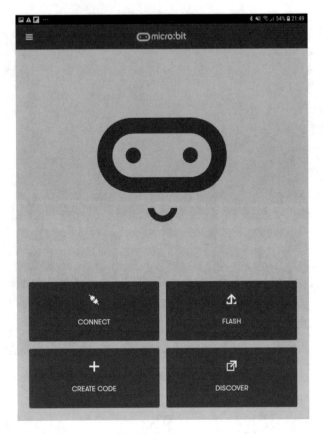

Figure 7-18. *The official micro:bit app. It is available for Android and iOS operating systems*

As an example, you can access the photo-/video-taking functionality of a remote device using the **tell camera to** block. In this section, you will build a simple project to take a photo with your **front camera** by pressing a Wearic textile pushbutton.

To build the circuit, you will need the following things:

- **micro:bit** – Provides a microprocessor and a Bluetooth radio

- **2 × AAA battery pack** – Powers your micro:bit after removing the micro USB cable from the computer

- **Micro USB cable** – Allows you to flash code onto the micro:bit

- **Wearic textile pushbutton double** – You can use whatever button you like (left or right)

- **10 KΩ resistor** – Helps to pull down pin 1

- **Alligator leads** – To connect things together

First, build the hardware using the above-mentioned things. Figure 7-19 shows the hardware setup.

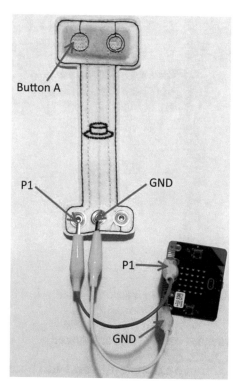

Figure 7-19. *Connecting the textile push-button element's button A with the micro:bit pin 1*

Then you should download the extension named **devices** onto your MakeCode project:

- Create a new MakeCode project and then go to the **Extensions** page. In the Extensions page, type **devices** in the search box and then press Enter (Figure 7-20).

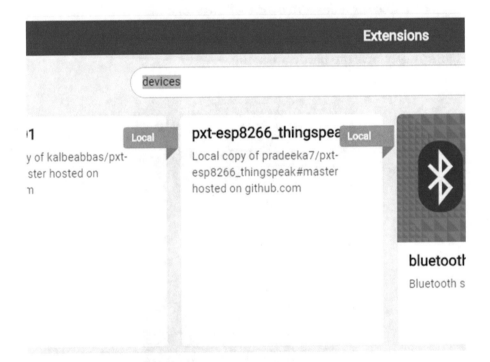

Figure 7-20. *Searching for the "devices" extension*

- From the search results, select **devices**.

- Click the **Remove extension(s) and add bluetooth** button (Figure 7-21). This is a mandatory step. You can't keep both the **radio** and **devices** extensions together because they will make conflicts (the "devices" extension is a type of Bluetooth extension).

Some extensions will be removed

Extension radio is incompatible with bluetooth. Remove radio and add bluetooth?

Remove extension(s) and add bluetooth ✔   Cancel ✖

Figure 7-21. *Removing the radio extension*

- From the search results, select **devices** (Figure 7-22).

- The devices extension will download onto your project.

Figure 7-22. *The "devices" extension*

Now you can start coding your camera button. The code is very simple, and you just need a few blocks. Table 7-2 shows the steps that you can follow to build the code.

Table 7-2. *Step-by-step instructions to build the code*

Step	MakeCode Blocks	Description
1	on pin P1 ▼ pressed / tell camera to launch photo mode ▼	*Place the **tell camera to** block into the **on pin P1 pressed** block. Then choose **launch photo mode** from the drop-down list.*
2	on pin P1 ▼ pressed / tell camera to launch photo mode ▼ / pause (ms) 5000 ▼	*Place the **pause** block into the **on pin P1 pressed** block. Then type 5000.*
3	on pin P1 ▼ pressed / tell camera to launch photo mode ▼ / pause (ms) 5000 ▼ / tell camera to take photo ▼	*Place another **tell camera to** block into the **on pin P1 pressed** block. Then choose **take photo** from the drop-down list.*

Figure 7-23 shows the full code created using the **MakeCode** blocks. You can also download the shared version of this code onto your editor by visiting **https://makecode.microbit.org/_5kyRmAdrhd1t**.

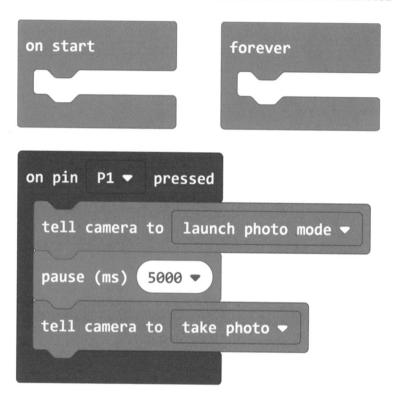

Figure 7-23. *Code for triggering camera through the Bluetooth*

After building the code, download and flash it onto your micro:bit. Now your micro:bit and the textile push-button element are ready. Finally download and install the official micro:bit app (Figure 7-24) on your smartphone or tablet.

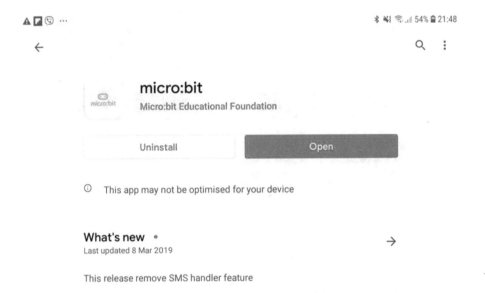

Figure 7-24. *The official micro:bit app download page at Google Play. Similar can be found at Apple App Store*

There are a few steps you should follow to pair your micro:bit with the micro:bit app:

- Power the micro:bit using a battery pack.

- Turn on **Bluetooth** (Figure 7-25) on your mobile device.

Figure 7-25. *Turning on the Bluetooth connectivity*

- Open the installed micro:bit app.

- Select the **CONNECT** button (Figure 7-26).

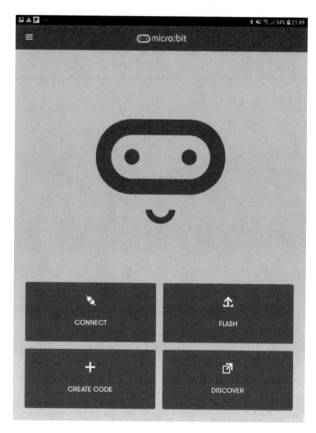

Figure 7-26. *Pairing the micro:bit – step 1*

- Click the **PAIR A NEW MICROBIT** button (Figure 7-27).

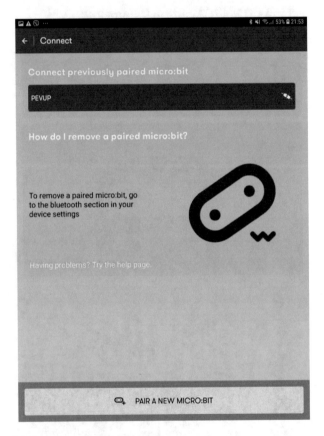

Figure 7-27. *Pairing the micro:bit – step 2*

- To pair your device with the micro:bit, press and hold down both buttons **A** and **B** and press the **RESET** button at the same time. Hold down the **RESET** button for 2 or 3 seconds and then release it. Then release buttons A and B. Click the **NEXT** button (Figure 7-28).

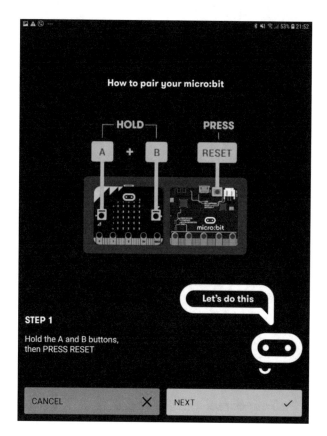

Figure 7-28. *Pairing the micro:bit – step 3*

- A pattern will appear on the micro:bit LED matrix. Draw the same pattern on the app's screen. Click the **PAIR** button (Figure 7-29).

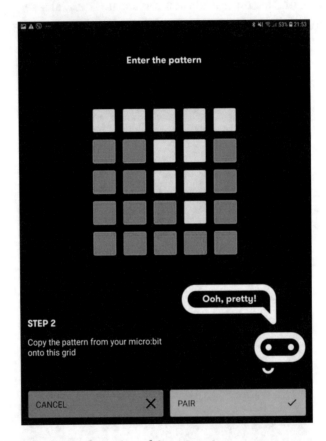

Figure 7-29. *Pairing the micro:bit – step 4*

- Press the **RESET** button on the micro:bit to finish the pairing process. Then select the **OK** button on the app (Figure 7-30).

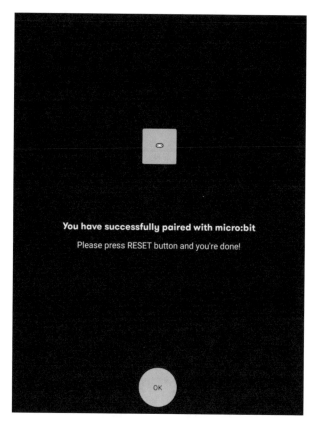

Figure 7-30. *Pairing the micro:bit – step 5*

- Now your micro:bit has been successfully paired with your mobile device. However, you need to connect your micro:bit with the app by selecting the name of your micro:bit (e.g., **PEVUP**) under **Connect previously paired micro:bit**. Also see the "disconnected plug" icon near the name of your micro:bit (Figure 7-31). Remember "pair" and "connect" are two different processes.

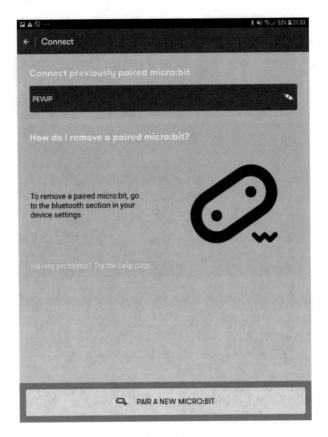

Figure 7-31. *Connecting the micro:bit*

- Now your micro:bit and the micro:bit app have been connected successfully. See the green plug icon near your micro:bit's name (Figure 7-32)

Figure 7-32. *micro:bit has been connected with the app*

Now you are ready to take photos with your smartphone or tablet:

- Place your smartphone/tablet wherever you want it to take the photo from.

- Press the **textile push-button A** on the micro:bit.

- Your **front camera** will turn on, and the timer will start.

- After 5 seconds, your camera will automatically take your photo. By default, your photo will be saved in the **Images/Camera** folder.

199

If you want to take a photo from the **rear camera** on your mobile device, simply modify the code as shown in Figure 7-33. You can also download the shared version of this code onto your editor by visiting `https://makecode.microbit.org/_88J9EmKq82jp`.

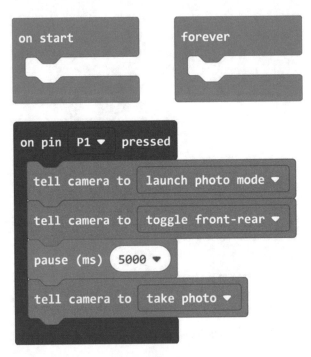

Figure 7-33. *MakeCode blocks to toggle rear camera to take photos*

7.7 Summary

In this chapter, you learned how to use the micro:bit's Bluetooth Low Energy feature to connect with your mobile device. With the BLE, you can send data to an app that supports the micro:bit, or you can control your phone with the micro:bit.

In the next chapter, you will learn how to add Internet connectivity to your micro:bit. You will learn real IoT with the micro:bit!

CHAPTER 8

Connecting Your Garments to the Internet with WiFi

In the previous chapter, you learned about sending data to a mobile app (micro:bit UART Terminal app) using the micro:bit's built-in Bluetooth Low Energy feature.

In this chapter, you'll be sending the Wearic pressure sensor data to the ThingSpeak IoT server using WiFi. This doesn't involve any intermediate app and provides fast, stable, and secure connectivity.

8.1 Building the WiFi Pressure Sensor

You will need the following things to build the WiFi pressure sensor:

- **micro:bit** – Works as the microprocessor

- **MuseLab micro:bit WiFi Booster** – Allows the micro:bit to connect to the Internet through WiFi (Figure 8-1)

© Pradeeka Seneviratne 2020
P. Seneviratne, *Beginning e-Textile Development*,
https://doi.org/10.1007/978-1-4842-6261-0_8

- **Three-pin generic connection cable** – Allows you to connect the Wearic pressure sensor to the WiFi booster. you will get with the WiFi booster.

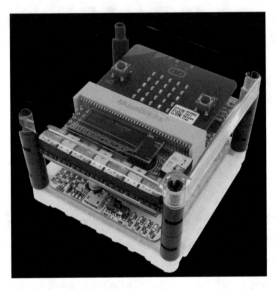

Figure 8-1. *micro:bit WiFi booster. Image courtesy of MuseLab* (`https://muselab.cc/product/muselab-microbit-booster/`

You can read more information about the MuseLab micro:bit WiFi Booster at `https://muselab.cc/product/muselab-microbit-booster/`.

- **micro USB cable** – Allows you to flash code onto the micro:bit

Before connecting anything to the micro:bit WiFi booster, make sure that the power switch on the "**multi-voltage power shield**" is in the **OFF** position. Then connect things to the micro:bit WiFi booster as explained in the following:

- Push the micro:bit to the edge connector of the WiFi booster.

- Connect the Wearic textile pressure sensor to the **P1**
  I/O port (you can use other ports too and update the
  code accordingly). The P1 I/O port has three pins,
  GND, 3.3V, and SIGNAL. The textile pressure sensor
  should connect between **3.3V** and the **SIGNAL** pins.
  Then connect **GND** and **SIGNAL** through a **10 KΩ**
  resistor to pull-down the pin (Figure 8-2).

Note   The P1 I/O port on the micro:bit WiFi booster internally
connects with the micro:bit P1.

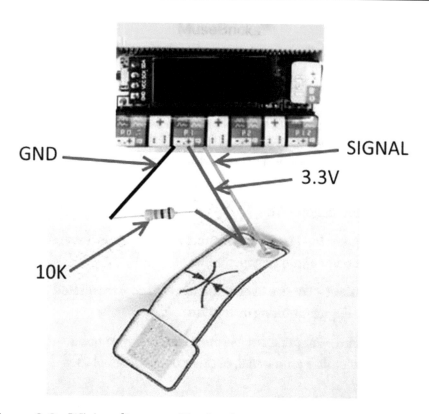

Figure 8-2. *Wiring diagram. Use hookup wires to connect alligator
leads with the WiFi booster*

- Now slide the power switch on the "**multi-voltage power shield**" to the ON position.

Now your hardware setup is ready, and you should program it to send data to the ThingSpeak IoT cloud.

8.2 Creating a ThingSpeak Account

As ThingSpeak says, "ThingSpeak is an IoT analytics platform service that allows you to aggregate, visualize, and analyze live data streams in the cloud." You can send data to ThingSpeak from your devices, create instant visualization of live data, and send alerts.

ThingSpeak is available as a free service that is suitable for non-commercial small projects under one of the following limitations:

- <3 million messages/year

- ~8,200 messages/day

As a commercial solution, ThingSpeak provides the following license types (listed here as mentioned on their website):

- **Standard** – For use at a commercial, government, or other organizations

- **Academic** – For use in teaching and academic research at a degree-granting institution

- **Student** – For use in conjunction with courses offered at a degree-granting institution

- **Home** – For personal use only. Not for government, academic, commercial, or other organizational uses

We will use the ThingSpeak free service because it provides a limit of 8200 messages per day. That is enough for our project because we will send sensor data every 5 seconds to ThingSpeak. To start using ThingSpeak, you must create a new MathWorks account. Follow the steps explained in the following to create a MathWorks account:

- Go to `https://thingspeak.com/`.

- Click the **Sign Up** button at the top right of the page (Figure 8-3).

Figure 8-3. *Sign Up button for ThingSpeak*

- Fill in the following fields (Figure 8-4):

  - **Email Address** – Any email address you own (Gmail works)

  - **Location** – Your country

  - **First Name** – Your first name

  - **Last Name** – Your last name

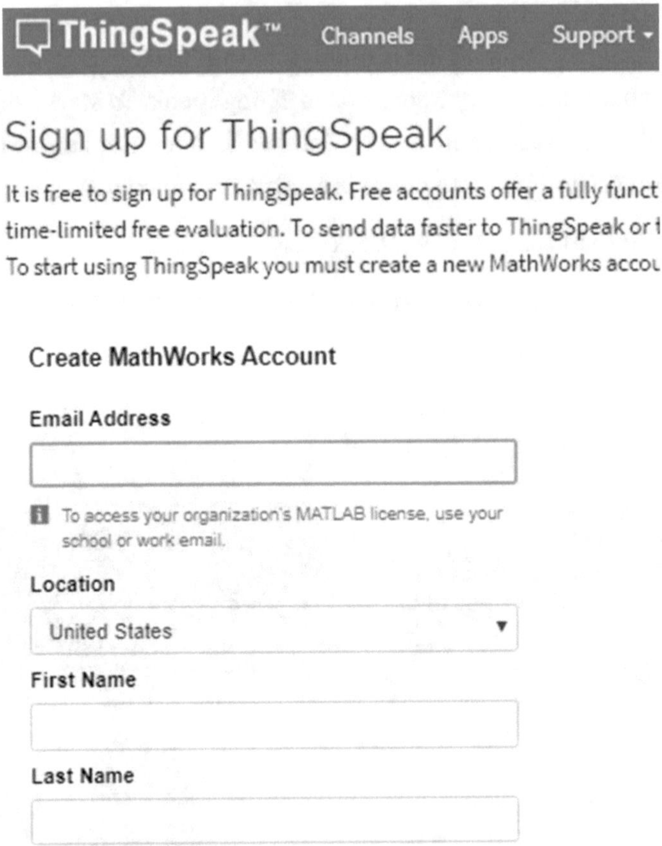

Figure 8-4. *"Create MathWorks Account" page*

- Click the **Continue** button (Figure 8-5).

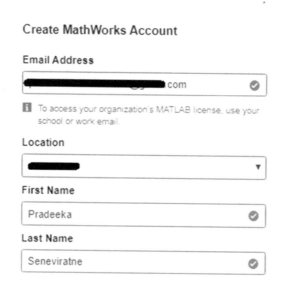

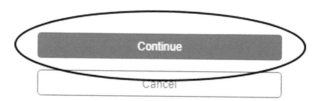

Figure 8-5. *Creating the account*

- You will get an error message about your email address. That's normal. First, click the checkbox next to the "**Use this email for my MathWorks account**," and then click again the **Continue** button (Figure 8-6).

Figure 8-6. *Continue anyway*

- You will get the following message. First, check if you have received an **email** from **MathWorks**. If yes, in the email, click the **Verify your email** button (Figure 8-7).

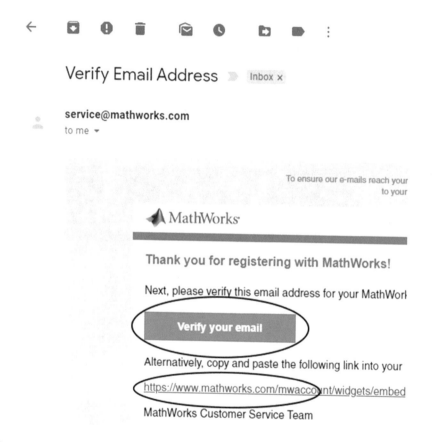

Figure 8-7. *Email for account verification*

- Then go to ThingSpeak and click the **Continue** button (Figure 8-8).

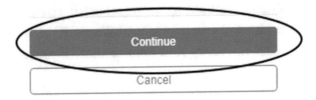

Figure 8-8. Continue with account creation

- If not, click the "**Send me the email again**" link. If that doesn't work for you, contact the customer support by clicking the "**Customer Support**" link (Figure 8-9).

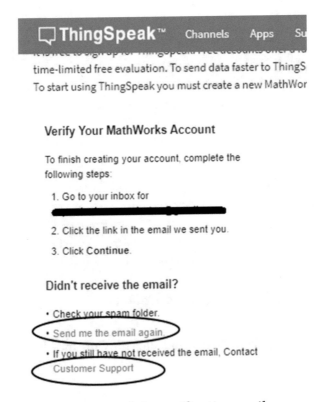

Figure 8-9. Request to resend the verification mail

- After successfully creating and verifying your account, you will get a message saying "**Your profile was verified**" (Figure 8-10).

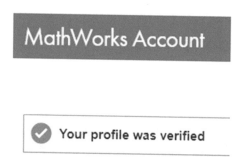

Figure 8-10. *A message saying that your profile was verified*

- Now you will get the "**Finish your Profile**" page (Figure 8-11). You should provide a user id and a password. Then click the **Continue** button.

Figure 8-11. *Providing a user id and a password*

- Now your account is completely created, and you have logged in to ThingSpeak. Click the **OK** button (Figure 8-12).

Figure 8-12. *"Sign-up successful" message*

- Choose the option "**Personal, non-commercial projects**," and then click the OK button (Figure 8-13).

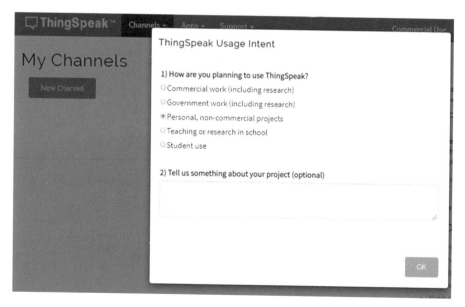

Figure 8-13. *Confirming the ThingSpeak usage intent*

8.3 Creating a ThingSpeak Channel

Now you should create a ThingSpeak channel to send your pressure sensor data. Follow these steps to create a channel:

- In the ThingSpeak **My Channels** page (**Channels ➤ My Channels**), click the **New Channel** button (Figure 8-14).

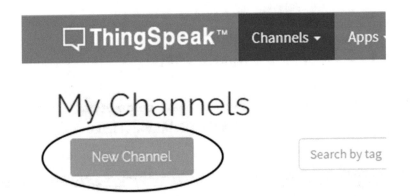

Figure 8-14. *Creating a new channel*

- In the New Channel page, fill the following fields (Figure 8-15):
  - **Name** – Chapter_8
  - **Description** – Displays textile pressure sensor data.
  - **Field 1** – pressure

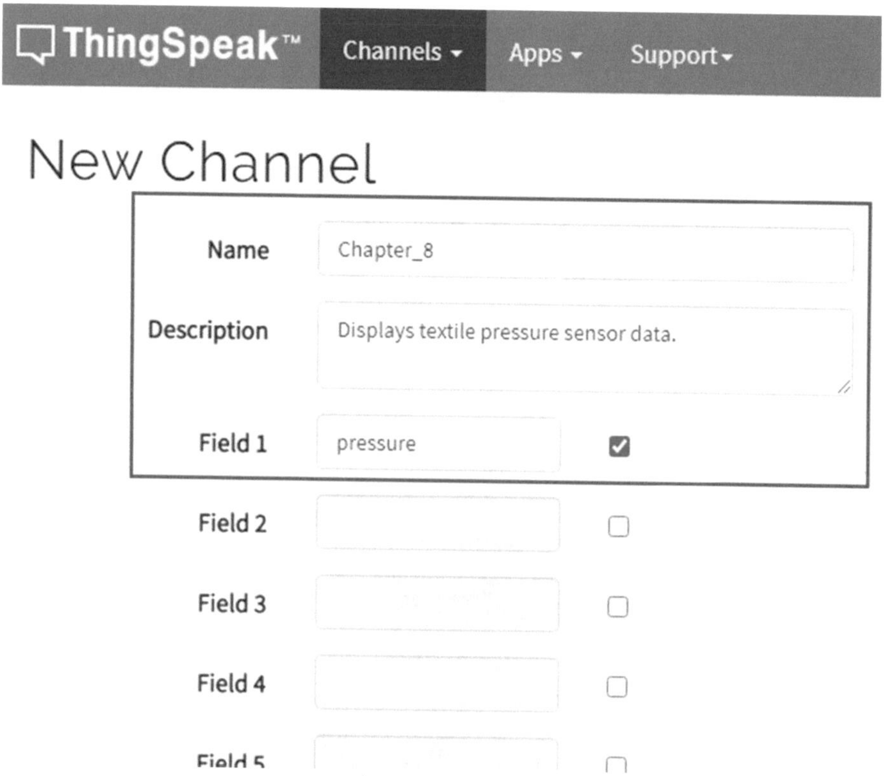

Figure 8-15. *Channel settings*

That's all. Leave the other fields as it is.

- Scroll down the page and click the **Save Channel** button (Figure 8-16).

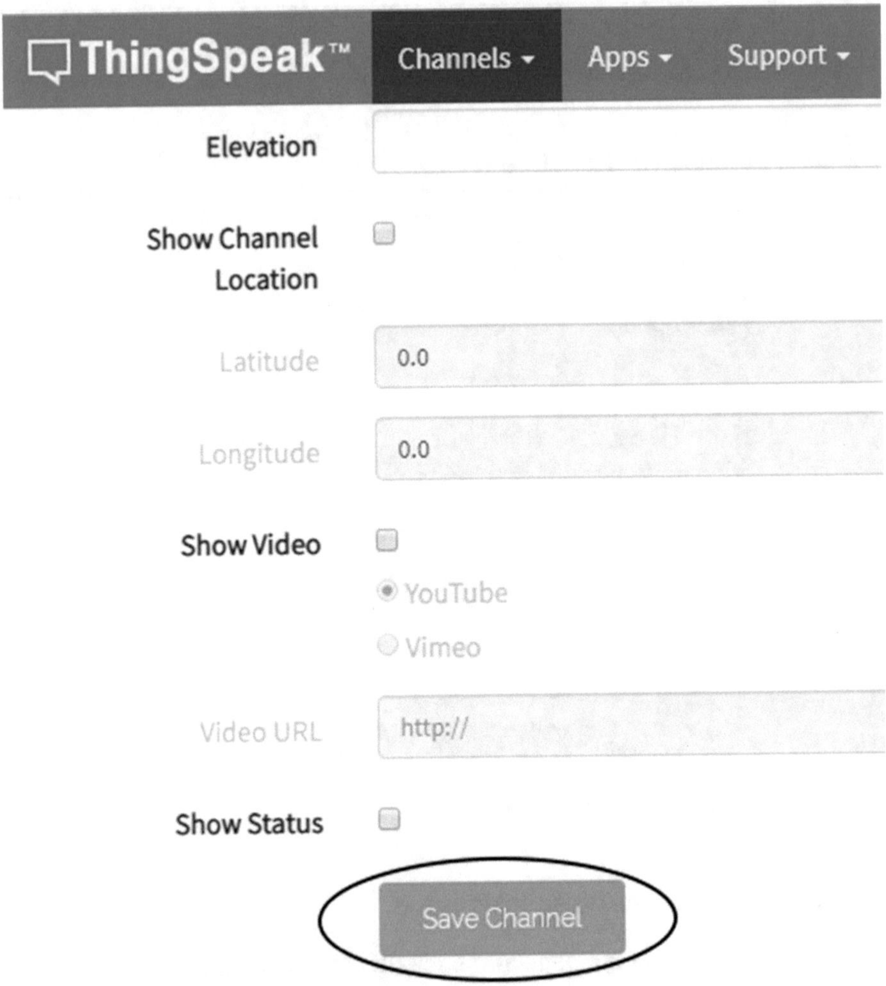

Figure 8-16. *Saving a channel*

- The channel has been created and displayed in the **My Channels** page (Figure 8-17).

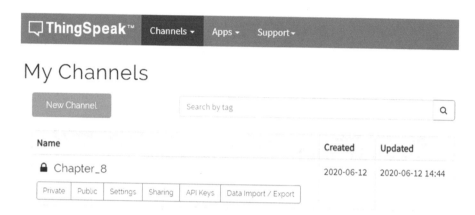

Figure 8-17. *My Channels page*

- Now click the **channel name** (Chapter_8). You can see
  a blank chart (Figure 8-18). Don't worry. In the next
  few sections, you will write and flash the code onto the
  micro:bit for sending data.

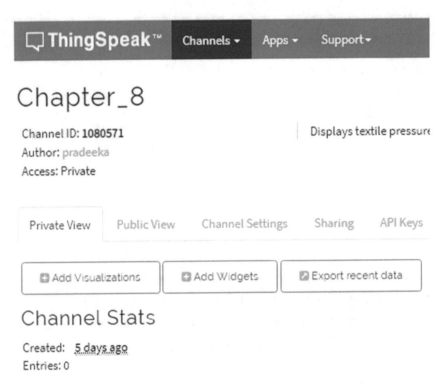

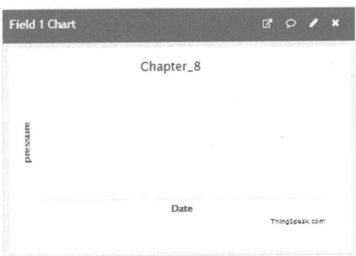

Figure 8-18. *Blank chart. No pressure sensor data available yet*

8.4 Downloading Muselab IoT Shield Extension

Before building the program with the MakeCode blocks, you should download the **Muselab IoT** Shield (a.k.a. **wifi-shield**) extension on to the MakeCode editor.

- In the Editor controls, click the **cogwheel** icon (Figure 8-19).

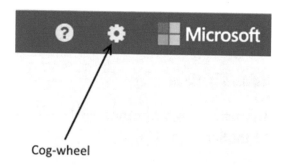

Cog-wheel

Figure 8-19. *Cogwheel icon*

- In the drop-down menu, click **Extensions** (Figure 8-20).

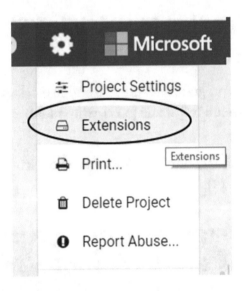

Figure 8-20. *Extensions menu*

- In the **Extensions** page, type **muselab** (Figure 8-21) and click the **Search** button.

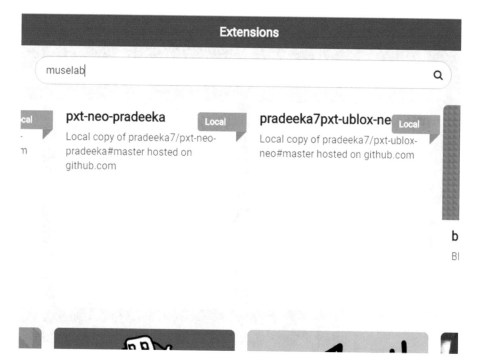

Figure 8-21. *Extensions page*

- The **Muselab wifi-shield** extension will show on the search result (Figure 8-22). Now click it to add to your project.

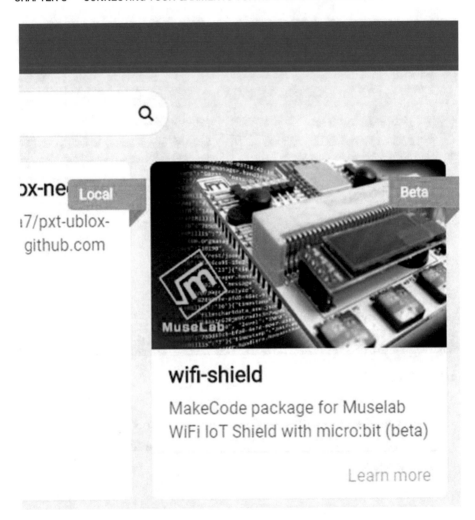

Figure 8-22. *MakeCode extension for Muselab WiFi IoT shield*

- It will take some time to download the extension to your project. Once downloaded, it can be found in the toolbox. The Muselab wifi-shield extension creates six toolbox drawers (Figure 8-23).

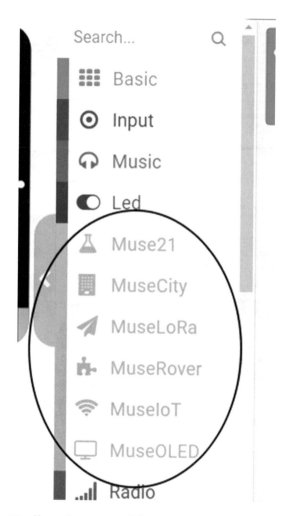

Figure 8-23. *Toolbox drawers of the Muselab extension*

- Among them, we will be using the **MuseIoT** toolbox
  drawer to build our code (Figure 8-24).

Figure 8-24. *MuseIoT toolbox drawer*

8.5 Coding the WiFi Pressure Sensor

Now you have set up all the things required to build the code. The following steps will guide you in detail on how to build the code with MakeCode blocks:

- Open the **MuseIoT** toolbox drawer. Drag out the **Initialize Muselab WiFi Booster** block onto the workspace, and place it into the **on start** block (Figure 8-25).

Figure 8-25. *Step 1*

- Open the **Basic** toolbox drawer. Drag out the **pause (ms)** block onto the workspace, and place it into the **on start** block under the **Initialize Muselab WiFi Booster and OLED** block. Then in the **pause (ms)** block, type in **5000** (Figure 8-26). This will tell micro:bit to wait for 5 seconds and execute the next block.

Figure 8-26. *Step 2*

- Open the **MuseIoT** toolbox drawer. Drag out the **Set wifi** block onto the workspace, and place it into the **on start** block after the **pause (ms)** block (Figure 8-27).

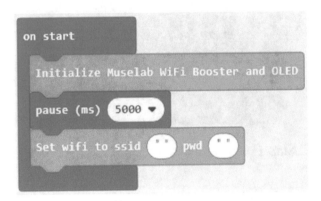

Figure 8-27. *Step 3*

- Type in **SSID** and **password** of the WiFi network you are going to connect with. If you have a home WiFi network, the **SSID** and password can be found on the router (Figure 8-28).

Figure 8-28. *Finding SSID and the password to connect to the WiFi router*

- After filling **SSID** and the password, the **Set wifi** block looks like that in Figure 8-29.

Figure 8-29. *Step 4*

- Open the **MuseIoT** toolbox drawer. Drag out the **Send Thingspeak** block onto the workspace, and place it into the **forever** block (Figure 8-30).

Figure 8-30. *Step 5*

- Find the **Write API Key** in your channel settings page (Figure 8-31).

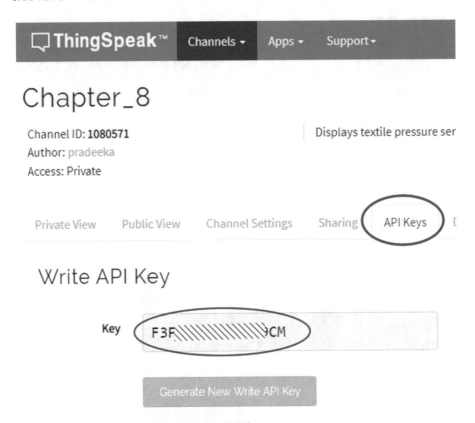

Figure 8-31. Finding the Write API key

- In the **key*** textbox, type in the ThingSpeak **Write API Key** (Figure 8-32).

Figure 8-32. Step 6

- Open the **Pins** toolbox drawer. Drag out the **analog read pin** block onto the workspace and place it into the **field1** of the **Send Thingspeak** block. Then choose **P1** from the drop-down menu (Figure 8-33).

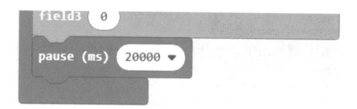

Figure 8-33. *Step 7*

- Open the **Basic** toolbox drawer. Drag out the **pause (ms)** block onto the workspace and place it into the **on start** block under the **Send Thingspeak** block. In the **pause (ms)** block, type **20000** (Figure 8-34). This will tell micro:bit to wait for 20 seconds and continue with the next cycle.

Note   For users of the free option, the message update interval limit remains limited at 15 seconds. So we will use 20 seconds for fair use.

Figure 8-34. *Step 8*

The completed code should look like as shown in Figure 8-35. You can also download the shared version of this code onto your editor by visiting `https://makecode.microbit.org/_3s1TiJAfYeuj` .

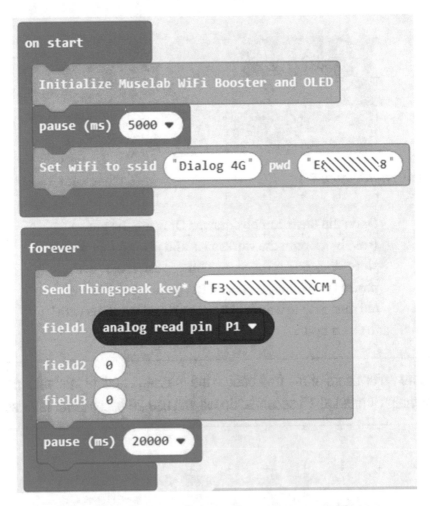

Figure 8-35. *Full code listing for sending pressure readings to ThingSpeak*

Now the code is completed and ready to flash onto your micro:bit. Connect the micro:bit with your computer using the micro USB cable. The following steps will guide you on how to compile and download the hex file onto your computer and flash it onto the micro:bit:

- In the project name box, type in a name for your project (first delete the default name, "Untitled") (Figure 8-36). The new name of the project will be updated in your browser's local cache.

Figure 8-36. *Providing a file name for the project*

- Click the **Download** button at the bottom of the editor page. A hex file will download to your computer (Figure 8-37).

Figure 8-37.   Downloaded hex file

- Drag and drop the hex file onto the micro:bit drive. The LED on the back of your micro:bit flashes during the transfer. Once this has completed, the micro:bit will automatically restart and start executing your code.

8.6 Visualizing the Data

Now you have completed everything, and it's time to visualize the pressure data with ThingSpeak:

- Go to your ThingSpeak channel and click the **Private View** tab. You can see the pressure data is coming from the micro:bit. Now using your fingers, apply some pressure onto the Wearic textile pressure sensor. You can see the pressure values get increased (Figure 8-38).

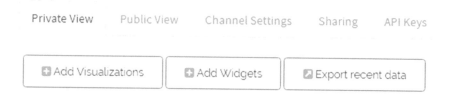

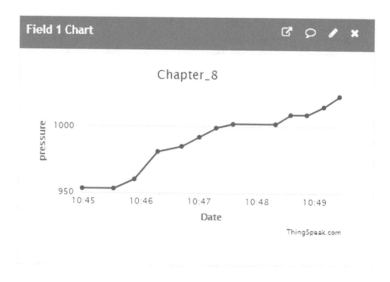

Figure 8-38. *Pressure sensor data is displaying on the chart*

8.7 Summary

In this chapter, you learned how to send pressure sensor data to the ThingSpeak IoT cloud through WiFi. The same thing can be applied to any type of sensor. Alternatively, you can modify the code to send data to **data.muselab.cc** (http://data.muselab.cc/), **IFTTT** (https://ifttt.com/), or **ArcGIS** (www.arcgis.com/index.html/).

Index

Printed in the United States
By Bookmasters